CU00427838

STUDENT UNIT GUIDE

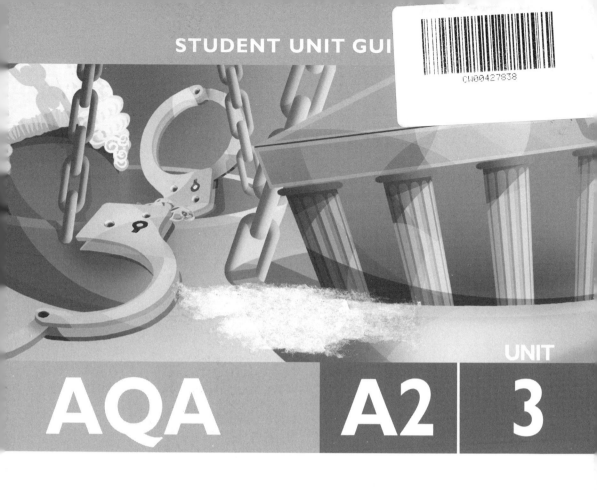

AQA | A2 | UNIT 3

Law

Criminal Law (Offences Against the Person)
and Contract Law

Ian Yule and Peter Darwent

510670

Philip Allan Updates, an imprint of Hodder Education, an Hachette UK company, Market Place, Deddington, Oxfordshire OX15 0SE

Orders

Bookpoint Ltd, 130 Milton Park, Abingdon, Oxfordshire OX14 4SB
tel: 01235 827720
fax: 01235 400454
e-mail: uk.orders@bookpoint.co.uk

Lines are open 9.00 a.m.–5.00 p.m., Monday to Saturday, with a 24-hour message answering service. You can also order through the Philip Allan Updates website: www.philipallan.co.uk

© Philip Allan Updates 2009

ISBN 978-0-340-95803-2

First printed 2009
Impression number 5 4 3 2 1
Year   2014 2013 2012 2011 2010 2009

All rights reserved; no part of this publication may be reproduced, stored in a retrieval system, or transmitted, in any other form or by any means, electronic, mechanical, photocopying, recording or otherwise without either the prior written permission of Philip Allan Updates or a licence permitting restricted copying in the United Kingdom issued by the Copyright Licensing Agency Ltd, Saffron House, 6–10 Kirby Street, London EC1N 8TS.

This guide has been written specifically to support students preparing for the AQA A2 Law Unit 3 examination. The content has been neither approved nor endorsed by AQA and remains the sole responsibility of the authors.

AQA examination questions are reproduced by permission of the Assessment and Qualifications Alliance.

Typeset by Phoenix Photosetting, Chatham, Kent
Printed by MPG Books, Bodmin

Hachette UK's policy is to use papers that are natural, renewable and recyclable products and made from wood grown in sustainable forests. The logging and manufacturing processes are expected to conform to the environmental regulations of the country of origin.

RESOURCE CENTRE
ST IVO SCHOOL
ST IVES

P1496

Contents

Introduction

About this guide 4

How to use this guide.. 4

Learning strategies 5

Revision planning... 5

■ ■ ■

Content Guidance

About this section 8

Section A: Criminal law (offences against the person)

Non-fatal offences against the person 9

Fatal offences against the person 10

Defences 23

Critical evaluation of law on offences against the person.................................... 33

Section B: Contract law

Formation of contract.. 42

Contract terms 47

Misrepresentation 54

Discharge of contract.. 57

Critical evaluation of contract law... 60

■ ■ ■

Questions and Answers

About this section 68

Section A

Q1 Non-fatal offence against the person 69

Q2 GBH and involuntary manslaughter 71

Q3 Critical evaluation of law on non-fatal offences.. 75

Section B

Q1 Misrepresentation and breach of contract 77

Q2 Frustration and breach of contract... 80

Q3 Offer and acceptance 82

Q4 Sale of Goods Act, exclusion clauses and privity of contract 85

Q5 Critical evaluation of law on offer and acceptance 88

Introduction

About this guide

The AQA specification for the A2 Law examinations is divided into two units. This guide covers Unit 3. Section A is Criminal Law (Offences against the Person) and Section B is Contract Law. For each section, the examination offers two three-part questions, and from these you select just one question to answer. The first two parts of each question are based on a scenario, and deal with substantive law issues; the third part is evaluative, and you are required to analyse aspects of either criminal law or contract law to consider potential criticisms, and possibly to suggest how the law could be reformed.

For the substantive law part of the module, it is vital to use case law effectively, and in the Questions and Answers section of this guide, you will be shown how best to employ case and statutory references.

How to use this guide

This guide is divided into two sections: Content Guidance and Questions and Answers. The Content Guidance section sets out the specification content for this unit, breaking it down into manageable areas for study and learning. It also contains references to case law to enable a fuller understanding of each topic. This section is not intended to be a comprehensive and detailed set of notes for this unit. You will need to supplement this material with further reading from textbooks and case studies.

The Questions and Answers section encourages you to test yourself. If you practise answering the sample questions and then assess your responses against the examiner's comments, you will learn how to use your knowledge and understanding more effectively to obtain high exam marks.

The key to doing well in the criminal law part of this unit lies in acquiring the ability to identify the appropriate offences and defences, and then defining the *actus reus* and *mens rea* of these, plus the defence requirements, and finally using relevant cases. For contract law, you need to be able to identify relevant issues on offer, acceptance, breach and remedies. To demonstrate a sound understanding of potential content, you need to practise answering past examination questions.

It is particularly important that you are able to apply legal rules to the specific scenario-based questions. This has been identified as a key examination weakness in successive examiner's reports.

Learning strategies

For successful A-level study, it is crucial to build up a good set of notes. These notes need to be laid out clearly under the headings used in the Content Guidance section and should contain accurate definitions and explanations, together with relevant case and statutory references. It is also recommended that you compile summaries of the most important cases, because this will make them much easier to remember and to use in examination answers.

Both AS and A2 examinations require you to appreciate the need to study independently, which means further reading from a wide variety of different sources and note-taking. Detailed case studies are also essential.

Revision planning

At this level of study, it is essential that you understand the need to learn basic factual information thoroughly. This should be done as the module is being taught. Do not leave it to the revision stage, because you will find there is simply too much detailed knowledge to absorb then.

The word 'revise' is defined in the *Concise Oxford Dictionary* as 'to read again (work learnt or done) to improve one's knowledge'. Skimming over some notes, or this Unit Guide, when you have not already learned the material is *not* revision.

The first stage of revision requires organisation of all your work. Ensure that:
- your class notes are up to date
- you have used the material in this Unit Guide effectively
- you have made accurate notes on any wider reading, especially case studies

You should then prepare a summary of all this material, organised under the headings and sub-headings of the unit specification. The revision period is the time to go over all your notes and reduce them to manageable proportions. This is, in itself, an effective learning exercise. By summarising the material, you should find it easier to learn, and there is less chance of you forgetting key information in the examination. The greatest number of exam marks are usually lost through simply forgetting to give fuller explanation and, in this unit particularly, through failing to show knowledge of relevant cases and to apply relevant legal rules to the question scenario.

Content Guidance

The specification for Unit 3 outlined in this section is as follows:

Section A: Criminal law (offences against the person)

Non-fatal offences against the person
- Summary of non-fatal offences
- Joint Charging Standard

Fatal offences against the person
- Murder
- Voluntary manslaughter
- Involuntary manslaughter

Defences
- Consent
- Insanity
- Automatism
- Self-defence
- Mistake
- Intoxication

Critical evaluation of law on offences against the person
- Critical evaluation of the law on non-fatal offences
- Critical evaluation of the law on fatal offences
- Critical evaluation of defences

Section B: Contract law

Formation of contract
- Offer
- Acceptance
- Consideration
- Invitations to treat
- Privity of contract
- Intention to create legal relations

Contract terms
- Conditions and warranties
- Express terms
- Implied terms
- Exemption clauses

Misrepresentation
- Statement of fact
- Inducing a party to enter a contract
- Types of misrepresentation
- Remedies for misrepresentation
- Exclusion of liability for misrepresentation

Discharge of contract
- Performance
- Agreement
- Frustration
- Breach

Critical evaluation of contract law
- Offer and acceptance
- Consideration
- Intention to create legal relations
- Contract terms
- Misrepresentation
- Remedies

Criminal law (offences against the person)

Non-fatal offences against the person

Summary of non-fatal offences

These should be revised from Unit 2.

Crime	Actus reus	Mens rea	Cases	Maximum sentence
Assault (common-law crime)	Causing victim to fear immediate, unlawful personal violence	Intention or subjective recklessness to causing *actus reus*	*Logdon v DPP* (1976) *R v Ireland* and *R v Constanza* (1997)	6 months or £5,000 fine
Battery (common-law crime)	Inflicting unlawful personal violence	Intention or subjective recklessness as to inflicting unlawful personal violence	*R v Fagan* (1968) *R v Thomas* (1985)	6 months or £5,000 fine
Section 47 ABH	Assault or battery causing actual bodily harm	Intention or recklessness as to the assault or battery	*R v Miller* (1954) *R v Chan-Fook* (1994) *R v Savage* and *R v Parmenter* (1992) *R v Roberts* (1971)	5 years
Section 20 GBH/wounding	GBH: serious injury Wounding: all layers of skin must be broken	Intention or recklessness as to *some harm*	*JJC v Eisenhower* (1983) *DPP v Smith* (1961) *R v Mowatt* (1968) *R v Grimshaw* (1984)	5 years
Section 18 GBH with intent	Wounding or GBH as in s.20	Specific intent to cause GBH, or intent to resist lawful arrest	*R v Nedrick* (1986) *R v Woollin* (1998)	Life

Joint Charging Standard

The police and the Crown Prosecution Service have agreed a Joint Charging Standard (see summary table on p. 10) to clarify what charges should be brought following different levels of injuries. However, it is important that you can also identify other potential offences with which those causing the particular injuries could also be charged.

Section 39: common assault (battery)	Section 47: assault occasioning ABH	Section 18 or Section 20: GBH or wounding
Grazes or scratches	Loss or breaking of tooth	Injury causing permanent disability or disfigurement
Abrasions	Temporary loss of consciousness	Broken limbs or bones
Minor bruising	Extensive or multiple bruising	Dislocated joints
Swelling	Displaced broken nose	Injuries causing substantial loss of blood
Reddening of the skin	Minor fractures	Injuries resulting in lengthy treatment
Superficial cuts	Minor cuts requiring stitches	Serious psychiatric injury — more than fear, distress or panic and requiring specialist treatment
A black eye	Psychiatric injury — more than fear, distress or panic	

Fatal offences against the person

Murder

Murder is the most serious crime against the person, and the offender, if convicted, will receive a mandatory life sentence. Murder is defined as 'unlawful killing with malice aforethought'. The *actus reus* is unlawful killing and the *mens rea* — malice aforethought — is more clearly defined as intention to kill or commit grievous bodily harm (GBH).

Actus reus

The *actus reus* often requires the examination of various rules of causation, in order to establish whether the defendant caused or brought about the death of the victim, hence the need to revise this topic thoroughly from Unit 2.

Mens rea

The *mens rea* for murder is malice aforethought, meaning intention to kill or commit GBH. The meaning of intention is not found in any statute but in judicial decisions. It is clear that a person intends a result when it is his or her aim, objective or purpose to bring it about — this is what might be termed 'dictionary intention'. In *R v Mohan* (1976), James LJ stated:

An 'intention', to my mind, connotes a state of affairs which the party intending ... does more than merely contemplate. It connotes a state of affairs which, on the contrary, he decides, so far as in him lies, to bring about, and which, in point of possibility, he has a reasonable prospect of being able to bring about by his own act of volition.

In a well-known hypothetical case, a person places a bomb in an aircraft with the intention that it will explode when the plane reaches an altitude of 20,000 feet. His specific aim or objective is to obtain the insurance money on the value of the lost aircraft. In these circumstances, he surely knows that when the plane explodes, all the passengers and crew will be killed, but does he actually intend their deaths? This type of case is one of 'oblique intent'.

In the case of R v Hancock and Shankland (1986), this issue was at the heart of the case. The judges had to decide how the law should deal with a defendant who has created an unlawful result where it is clear that the outcome was probable — even highly probable — and the defendant may well have foreseen this outcome. In this case, the defendants were Welsh coal miners on strike. When one of their fellow miners wanted to return to work, they tried to stop the 'strike-breaker' as he was being driven to another coal mine in a taxi. When the taxi passed under a motorway bridge, the other miners threw down rocks and pieces of the bridge, and one of the larger rocks smashed through the windscreen, killing the driver. Clearly the miners had killed the taxi driver and, had they been charged with manslaughter, they would have pleaded guilty. However, the charge was murder, which requires an intention to kill or commit serious injury. The defendants denied having such an intention, admitting that their intention was only to prevent the strike-breaker from reaching the coal mine.

They were convicted of murder at their trial, but the Court of Appeal and House of Lords both quashed those convictions and substituted manslaughter convictions, holding that the issue of intention had not been established. Lord Scarman indicated that, in cases like these, juries needed to be told by the judge that 'the greater the probability of a consequence occurring, the more likely it was so foreseen and, if so, the more likely it was intended'. This emphasised that foresight of a degree of probability was only evidence from which intention could be inferred.

In the more recent cases of R v Nedrick (1986) and R v Woollin (1998), a tighter rule was laid down for such cases of oblique intent. This rule provides that juries may return a verdict of murder only where they find that 'the defendant foresaw death or serious injury as a virtually certain consequence of his or her voluntary actions'. In both these cases, the original murder conviction was substituted on appeal by a manslaughter conviction.

In R v Woollin (1998), the defendant initially gave a number of different explanations, but finally admitted that he had 'lost his cool' when his 3-month-old baby son started to choke on his food. He had shaken the baby and then, in a fit of rage or frustration, had thrown him in the direction of his pram, which was standing against the wall about a metre away. He knew that the baby's head had hit something hard but denied intending to throw him against the wall or wanting him to die or suffer serious injury. The trial judge directed the members of the jury that they might infer intention if they were satisfied that, when the defendant threw the baby, he appreciated there was a 'substantial risk' of causing serious harm. On appeal, the defendant argued that the judge should have used the words 'virtual certainty', as 'substantial risk' was merely a test of recklessness. Although critical of the trial judge, the Court of Appeal dismissed the appeal, and certified questions for the House of Lords.

The House of Lords quashed the conviction for murder and substituted a conviction for manslaughter. Lord Steyn, who gave the main speech, declared that 'the effect of the [trial judge's] critical direction is that a result foreseen as virtually certain is an intended result'. The phrase 'substantial risk', used by the trial judge, blurred the distinction between intention and recklessness and was too serious a misdirection for the conviction to stand. In *R v Matthews and Alleyne* (2003), the vexed issue of whether foresight of virtually certain consequences was equivalent to intent or was merely evidence of it was resolved in favour of its being evidential.

Voluntary manslaughter

Voluntary manslaughter covers the situation where the defendant has committed the *actus reus* of murder (unlawful killing) with the required *mens rea* (specific intention to kill or commit GBH) but there are extenuating circumstances that reduce the defendant's liability. These circumstances operate as partial defences, and are defined as provocation or diminished responsibility. Uniquely, the defendant is not charged with the offence of voluntary manslaughter but with murder, to which he or she will plead the relevant defence. If successful, he or she will then be convicted of manslaughter. These partial defences, important as they are now when there is a mandatory life sentence for murder, were even more important before 1963, when they operated as 'gallows savers', because then the mandatory penalty for murder was death by hanging.

The basis of all serious criminal liability — the liability to be prosecuted and, if convicted, to be punished — rests on the principle of fault. In the case of these partial defences, which can only be pleaded to a murder charge, the law recognises that, in some way, the defendant's fault has been reduced and therefore he or she is entitled to receive a lower punishment than life imprisonment. This reduced fault may be established:

- through proof that the defendant suffered from an abnormality of mind that 'substantially impaired' his mental responsibility for the killing
- where the defendant lost self-control because of provocation and 'the reasonable man' would also have lost self-control and reacted by killing

These partial defences are defined in the **Homicide Act 1957**.

Diminished responsibility

Section 2(1) of the **Homicide Act 1957** states:

> Where a person kills or is a party to the killing of another, he shall not be convicted of murder if he was suffering from such abnormality of mind (whether arising from a condition of arrested or retarded development...or induced by disease or injury) as substantially

impaired his mental responsibility for his acts and omissions in doing or being a party to the killing.

This partial defence was introduced into English law from Scottish law where, in *H. M. Advocate* v *Braithwaite* (1945), the Lord Justice Clerk, Lord Cooper, defined it as 'bordering on, but not amounting to, insanity'. In *Galbraith* v *H. M. Advocate (No. 2)* (2002), it was redefined as an abnormality of mind that substantially impaired a defendant's ability to determine or control conduct for which he or she would otherwise be convicted of murder.

A leading English case is that of *R* v *Byrne* (1960), where the defendant suffered from perverted sexual desires, which created impulses he found it impossible to control. Here, Lord Parker CJ stated that 'an abnormality of mind is a state of mind so different from that of ordinary human beings that the reasonable man would term it abnormal'. He went on to stress that, once the jury is satisfied that the defendant was suffering from an abnormality of mind, it must then be satisfied that this abnormality was 'significant enough to substantially impair his mental responsibility for his acts'. Note that, as with a defence of insanity, the burden of proof rests with the defendant. He or she has to prove both elements of this defence — but by the civil standard of proof, which is the balance of probabilities.

The required abnormality of mind has been held to include severe shock or depression, especially in cases of mercy killing. In *R* v *Hobson* (1997), the Court of Appeal accepted that 'battered woman's syndrome' was a mental disease and could thus cause an abnormality of mind. In order to satisfy s.2 and for the defence to succeed, the abnormality of mind must have substantially impaired the defendant's mental responsibility.

The impairment of control need not be complete, but it must be considerable. In *R* v *Byrne*, there was evidence that the impulses from which the defendant suffered were not absolutely irresistible, but were extremely difficult to control. In that case, this was considered sufficient, but it will always be a matter for the jury to decide. In *R* v *Lloyd* (1967), it was held that for it to be substantial, 'the impairment need not be total but it must be more than trivial or minimal'.

Where intoxication has produced an abnormality of the mind, for example the brain has been damaged because the defendant is an alcoholic, then the defence of diminished responsibility could be established. However, for alcohol simply to have had a transitory effect on the mind would not be enough to trigger the defence. In the leading case of *R* v *Tandy* (1989), the Court of Appeal held that for alcohol to produce an abnormality of mind:

> ...the alcoholism had to have reached such a level that the defendant's brain was damaged so that there was gross impairment of his judgement and emotional responses or the craving for drink had to be such as to render the defendant's use of drink involuntary because he was no longer able to resist the impulse to drink.

However, in *R* v *Wood* (2008), Judge LJ argued that, 'as a matter of practical reality the bar the defendant is required to surmount before diminished responsibility can be established in the context of chronic addiction to alcohol may have been set too high' in

R v *Tandy*, and that, 'nothing in s.2 itself suggests that alcohol dependency syndrome [alcoholism] is excluded from consideration as a possible source of abnormality of mind'. He concluded by deciding that this defence, when arising as a result of alcohol consumption, was a jury matter, and the test was whether or not it had been established that the defendant's syndrome was of such an extent and nature that it constituted an abnormality of mind induced by illness or disease. If it was, then the defence was available, subject to the jury then considering whether the defendant's craving for alcohol was irresistible or not. The fact that some alcohol was consumed voluntarily would not necessarily deprive the defendant of this defence.

Note the case of *R* v *Dietschmann* (2003), where the defendant had killed his victim while intoxicated *and* suffering from an abnormality of mind. It was held (following the 1984 case of *R* v *Gittens*) that, where a defendant charged with murder was suffering from an abnormality of mind and had also consumed alcohol (and where, as in this case, there was no evidence capable of establishing alcohol dependence syndrome as an abnormality of mind), if he or she satisfies the jury that, notwithstanding the alcohol he or she had consumed and its effect upon him or her, his or her abnormality of mind substantially impaired his or her mental responsibility for his or her acts in doing the killing, the jury should find the defendant not guilty of murder but guilty of voluntary manslaughter by reason of diminished responsibility.

In referring to substantial impairment of mental responsibility, s.2 of the **Homicide Act 1957** does not require the abnormality of mind to be the sole cause of the defendant's acts in doing the killing. Therefore, even if the defendant would not have killed if he or she had not consumed alcohol, the causative effect of the drink does not necessarily prevent an abnormality of mind suffered by him or her from substantially impairing his or her mental responsibility for the fatal acts. The cases of *R* v *Atkinson* (1985) and *R* v *Egan* (1992) were wrongly decided, insofar as they hold that a defence of diminished responsibility is not available if the defendant cannot show that he or she would have killed, even if he or she had not taken drink. A jury should be directed that alcohol cannot be taken into account as something that contributed to mental impairment within s.2 and to any impairment of mental responsibility arising from that abnormality, but that a defendant should be convicted of voluntary manslaughter rather than murder on the grounds of diminished responsibility if he or she can satisfy the jury that, despite the alcohol, his or her mental abnormality substantially impaired the mental responsibility for the fatal acts.

Exam hints
- Do not refer to this defence except in murder cases, where the possibility of insanity could also be considered. For any offence other than murder, if there is any issue concerning any 'abnormality of mind', this can only be dealt with under insanity.
- With problem-solving exam questions involving diminished responsibility, candidates are required to identify the probable cause of this condition from the 'list' in s.2.

Provocation
Section 3 of the **Homicide Act 1957** states:

Where on a charge of murder there is evidence on which a jury can find that the person charged was provoked (whether by things done or by things said or by both together) to lose his self-control, the question whether the provocation was enough to make a reasonable man do as he did shall be left to be determined by the jury; and in determining that question the jury shall take into account everything both done and said according to the effect which, in their opinion, it would have on a reasonable man.

The criteria for establishing provocation, together with the supporting cases, are outlined below.

Evidence

There must be evidence capable of amounting to provocation, and this is decided by the judge. This is the limit of the judge's role, as the success or failure of this defence is left to the jury. Note that even if this defence has not been specifically led by lawyers for the defendant, provided there is some evidence of provocation, this must be put by the judge to the jury. See *R* v *Cambridge* (1994), and also *R* v *Acott* (1997), where it was held that, as there was no specific evidence of provocation but merely speculation, the trial judge was right not to direct the jury on the issue of provocation. This was confirmed in *R* v *Miao* (2003) and in *R* v *Serrano* (2006).

Things said and/or done

Today, provocation may result from things said, done or both, whereas before the **1957 Act** only things done could amount in law to provocation. In *R* v *Doughty* (1986), even the crying of a young baby was considered provocative. A court can also take into account cumulative provocation that has taken place over a long period of time (see the 1995 case of *R* v *Humphrey*). This means that the final provocation is considered not in isolation but in the context of all the provocative incidents that have gone before it.

Loss of self-control

The provocation must have caused the defendant to lose his or her self-control. If the defendant, although provoked, lost his or her self-control for any other reason, the defence fails. This involves something more than anger or a loss of temper. In *R* v *Duffy* (1949), Lord Devlin defined the effect of provocation as 'a sudden and temporary loss of self-control, rendering the defendant so subject to passion as to make him for the moment not the master of his mind'. Note that evidence of provocation followed by premeditated action will result in this defence being lost; see *R* v *Ibrams* (1981), where it was held that the existence of a 'cooling-off period' between the provocation and the killing was evidence that the loss of self-control was not 'sudden and temporary'. However, in *R* v *Baillie* (1995), the Court of Appeal ruled that the defence of provocation should have been put to the jury, even when the defendant, following the provocation, had gone into his attic to get a gun and had then driven his car for 2 miles and filled up with petrol before shooting his victim. It must also be noted that the existence of a cooling-off period is not a matter of law but a piece of evidence that the jury may use to decide whether or not, at the time of the killing, the defendant was deprived of self-control — see *R* v *Ahluwalia* (1992).

Induced provocation

Following *R* v *Johnson* (1989), it has been established that if the provocation was induced by the defendant in the first place, this does not necessarily prevent the defence being available. In this case, the defendant and his friend had been drinking when the defendant threatened violence towards both the friend and the friend's female companion. A struggle took place between the defendant and the friend, during which the defendant stabbed the friend to death with a flick-knife. His appeal against his murder conviction was allowed, as the judge had refused to allow the issue of provocation to be considered by the jury.

The 'reasonable man' test

For the defence of provocation to succeed, it must be proved that not only would a reasonable person have been provoked, but that such provocation would have made a reasonable person act as the defendant did: in other words, that the response was not out of all proportion to the provocation. See the contrasting cases of *R* v *Bedder* (1954) and *DPP* v *Camplin* (1978). Overruling *R* v *Bedder*, Lord Diplock stated in *DPP* v *Camplin* that the reasonable man:

> ...is a person having the power of self-control to be expected of an ordinary person of the sex and age of the defendant, but in other respects sharing such of the defendant's characteristics as [the jury] think would affect the gravity of the provocation to him.

In *R* v *Roberts* (1990), a 23-year-old man who suffered from substantial deafness and impaired speech killed someone as a result of taunts about his condition. It was held that the judge had rightly directed that the hypothetical reasonable person had those characteristics. Both *R* v *Ahluwalia* and *R* v *Thornton* (1992) have now confirmed that 'battered woman's syndrome' might constitute a relevant characteristic.

This objective test was stretched further in *R* v *Morhall* (1996), where the defendant was a glue-sniffer who was taunted by the victim about his addiction. A fight ensued and the defendant killed the other man. He was convicted of murder and appealed on the ground of provocation. The Court of Appeal rejected his submission on the basis that 'repugnant characteristics' could not be attributed to the 'reasonable man'. The House of Lords overturned this, holding that such characteristics could and should be taken into account when applying the objective test, provided that the characteristic in question was the target of the provocation — a 'response' characteristic, as opposed to the 'control' characteristics that merely have an effect on the defendant's ability to control himself or herself (see the 1997 case of *Luc Thiet Thuan* v *R*).

The controversial decision in *R* v *Smith* (2001) overturned the Privy Council decision in *Luc Thiet Thuan* v *R* and held that the question for the jury was whether it thought that, 'the behaviour of the defendant had measured up to the standard of self-control which ought reasonably to have been expected of him'. This decision was greatly criticised for blurring the distinction between the subjective and objective tests

In an article in the *New Law Journal* of 11 August 2000, Laurence Toczek wrote:

> Lord Hoffmann [in *R* v *Smith*] attempts to deal with the argument that, if there is no limit to the characteristics which can be taken into account, the objective element will disappear

completely. Lord Hoffmann agrees that this would be most undesirable. His solution is to suggest that judges should direct juries that characteristics such as jealousy and obsession should be ignored in relation to the objective element. (Lord Clyde adds 'exceptional pugnacity or excitability' to this list of excluded characteristics.)

This, according to the writer, creates an obvious problem: how is the line to be drawn between inadmissible characteristics of this sort and admissible characteristics such as Smith's depressive illness?

In *Attorney General for Jersey* v *Holley* (2005), a nine-judge panel of the Privy Council took the opportunity to 'clarify definitively the present state of English law on provocation'. Following a retrial at the Royal Court in Jersey, the defendant was convicted of murder. A chronic alcoholic, he admitted killing his girlfriend with an axe while under the influence of alcohol. The sole issue at trial was provocation. The Court of Appeal allowed his subsequent appeal and substituted a conviction for manslaughter, on the ground that the deputy bailiff had misdirected the jury on the issue of provocation. The Attorney General appealed to the Privy Council. Lord Nicholls gave the majority judgement of the nine-judge panel. The main focus of the judgement was the 'reasonable man test' in s.3 of the **Homicide Act 1957**. Lord Nicholls stated that:

[This] has been the most difficult issue in the whole law of provocation. It can be divided into two separate tests — the first calls for an assessment of the gravity of the provocation, the second then requires an application of an external standard of self-control — 'whether the provocation was enough to make a reasonable man do as he did'.

The first problem concerns the use of the words 'a reasonable man', for it is difficult to conceive of circumstances where it would be 'reasonable' for a person to respond to a taunt by killing his tormentor. Rather, the phrase is intended to refer to an ordinary person; that is, a person of ordinary self-control. In *DPP* v *Camplin*, Lord Diplock defined this person as 'an ordinary person of either sex, not exceptionally excitable or pugnacious, but possessed of such powers of self-control as everyone is entitled to expect that his fellow citizens will exercise'.

[The judge] should...explain to [the jury] that the reasonable man referred to...is the person having the power of self-control to be expected of an ordinary person of the sex and age of the accused, but in other respects sharing such of the accused's characteristics as they think would affect the gravity of provocation to him; and that the question is not merely whether such a person would in like circumstances be provoked to lose his self-control, but also whether he would react to the provocation as the accused did.

Lord Nicholls decisively overturned the majority judgement in *R* v *Smith* on the simple ground that 'the statute does not leave each jury free to set whatever standard they consider appropriate in the circumstances by which to judge whether the defendant's conduct is "excusable"'. He held that:

However much the contrary is asserted, the majority view [in *Smith*] does represent a departure from the law as declared in s.3 of the Homicide Act 1957. It involves a significant relaxation of the uniform, objective standard adopted by Parliament. Under the statute the sufficiency of the provocation is to be judged by one standard, not a standard which varies from defendant to defendant.

He further stated that the law on homicide:

> ...was a highly sensitive and controversial area of the criminal law. In 1957, Parliament altered the common law relating to provocation and declared what the law on the subject should be. In those circumstances, it was not open to judges now to change the common law and thereby depart from the law as declared by Parliament.

On the issue of diminished responsibility, it was clearly stated that, in such cases, the defendant should argue his or her case on the basis of diminished responsibility, not provocation, on the ground that 'statutory provision [s.2] represents the legislature's view on how cases of mental abnormality are to be accommodated in the law of homicide'. This was also the view of the Court of Appeal in *R* v *Ahluwalia*, where a defence of provocation failed and a retrial was ordered on the issue of diminished responsibility.

The decision in *Holley* was confirmed as correct by the Court of Appeal in the 2006 cases of *R* v *James* and *R* v *Karimi*, where the five appeal judges presided over by Lord Phillips CJ decided that the Privy Council decision should be followed rather than the House of Lords' decision in *R* v *Smith*; in effect, the Court of Appeal was saying that the Privy Council overruled the House of Lords. Finally, note that, for reasons of policy, intoxication cannot be taken into account because of the common law rule that it does not of itself excuse a person from committing a criminal offence; see *R* v *Newell* (1980).

Involuntary manslaughter

Involuntary manslaughter includes all types of homicide (unlawful killing) committed *without* malice aforethought (specific intention to kill or commit GBH). It has always been the most difficult of homicides to construe because its *mens rea* is defined in the negative. It has been observed by Lord Atkin that:

> ...of all crimes, manslaughter appears to afford most difficulties of definition, for it concerns homicide in so many and so varying conditions...the law...recognises murder on the one hand based mainly, though not exclusively, on an intention to kill, and manslaughter on the other hand, based mainly, though not exclusively, on the absence of intent to kill, but with the presence of an element of 'unlawfulness' which is the elusive factor.

A further source of difficulty is that, in a sense, manslaughter is caught between murder at the extreme end of criminal liability and accidental death at the other end, where no criminal liability usually attaches.

Currently, the law recognises three broad categories of involuntary manslaughter:
- manslaughter by an unlawful and dangerous act
- manslaughter by gross negligence
- reckless manslaughter

Manslaughter by unlawful and dangerous act

According to Smith and Hogan in *Criminal Law*:

> [A defendant] is guilty of manslaughter if he kills by an unlawful and dangerous act. The only *mens rea* required is an intention to do that act and any fault required to render it unlawful. It is irrelevant that the defendant is unaware that it is unlawful or that it is

dangerous, and that he is unaware of the circumstances which make it dangerous, if a reasonable person would have been aware of them.

Unlawful act

It is now established that for an act to be unlawful for the purposes of this offence, it must be a crime. A tort or breach of contract is not enough. In *R* v *Franklin* (1883), which involved the tort of trespass, the trial judge ruled: 'The mere fact of a civil wrong committed by one person against another ought not to be used as an incident which is a necessary step in a criminal case.' It seems to be settled law from the cases of *R* v *Lamb* (1967) and *R* v *Jennings* (1990) that a criminal act must be identified and proved, including the necessary *mens rea*. It was because no initial crime was proved to have been committed that Lamb's conviction was quashed on appeal. This was also the case in *R* v *Scarlett* (1993), where the defendant's conviction was quashed because the Crown had not been able to produce evidence that the defendant's use of force had been unreasonable and was therefore unlawful.

It is vital to understand that the *mens rea* for involuntary manslaughter is that of the initial crime — and it can be intention or recklessness. Although most cases involve some form of assault, which requires intention or subjective recklessness, in *DPP* v *Newbury and Jones* (1976), the initial offence (which was not identified in the case) was surely that of criminal damage, for which objective recklessness was required (see *MPC* v *Caldwell* 1982). However, the case of *R* v *G* (2003) has since abolished the requirement of objective recklessness in cases of criminal damage. As regards omission, it seems to be the case, following *R* v *Lowe* (1973), that if the omission is no more than an act of negligence, this will not be the basis of manslaughter by unlawful dangerous act unless the omission is truly wilful, for example a deliberate omission to summon emergency medical aid, knowing it to be necessary. Omissions that cause death should therefore be dealt with under the law on manslaughter by gross negligence.

Dangerous act

In *R* v *Church* (1966), Edmund-Davies J stated:

> For such a verdict to follow, the unlawful act must be such as all sober and reasonable people would inevitably recognise must subject the other person to, at least, the risk of some harm resulting therefrom, albeit not serious harm.

The test of dangerousness is therefore objective. In *DPP* v *Newbury* (1976), Lord Salmon stressed: 'The test is not that the defendant recognised that it was dangerous but would all sober and reasonable people recognise its danger.' The question is further extended to consider whether the reasonable person would have appreciated that the act was dangerous in the light not only of the circumstances actually known to the defendant, but also of any additional circumstances of which the hypothetical person would have been aware; see the leading case of *R* v *Watson* (1989), but note that the defendant's conviction for the manslaughter during a burglary of an 87-year-old man was overturned on appeal on the ground that causation had not been proved.

In *R* v *Dawson* (1985), where an armed robbery at a petrol station had led to the station attendant's death from a heart attack, the original conviction for manslaughter was quashed on appeal because, it seems, the court assumed that in the context of this offence, 'harm' includes 'injury to the person through the operation of shock emanating from fright'. As Professor J. C. Smith comments in *Criminal Law*: 'It seems that it is not enough that the act is likely to frighten. It must be likely to cause such shock as to result in physical injury.' The question arises, however, as to why the 'thin skull' rule (that defendants take their victims as they find them) was not applied in this case.

Causation

The unlawful and dangerous act must be the cause of the victim's death. At one time, it was considered that the act had to be directed at the victim, but following *R* v *Goodfellow* (1986), it is now clear that if the act satisfies both the normal factual and legal rules of causation, this will suffice for such a charge to be brought. This decision was confirmed by the House of Lords in *Attorney General's Reference (No. 3 of 1994)*, where it was held not only that there is no requirement for the unlawful act to be directed at the victim, but also that there is no requirement that the danger or risk of harm should be perceived in respect of the actual victim — a risk of harm to someone else arising from the unlawful act will suffice.

Manslaughter by gross negligence

Manslaughter by gross negligence is based on the civil tort of negligence and is most commonly the result of an omission — a failure to act where there is a clear duty to act (see *R* v *Stone and Dobinson*, 1977). The view of Lord Hewart CJ in *R* v *Bateman* (1925) is still important:

> In order to establish criminal liability, the facts must be such that in the opinion of the jury, the negligence of the accused went beyond a mere matter of compensation between subjects (civil tort liability) and showed such disregard for the life and safety of others as to amount to a crime against the state and conduct deserving punishment.

Duty of care

To obtain a conviction for manslaughter by gross negligence, the Crown must show that there is a duty of care owed by the defendant to the victim. This issue has caused considerable difficulty but, following *R* v *Adomako* (1994), it now appears that the duty of care is simply based on the 'neighbour' test in *Donoghue* v *Stevenson* (1932) or on the incremental approach in *Caparo Industries plc* v *Dickman* (1990). For both cases, see *Student Unit Guide AQA A2 Unit 4, Criminal Law (Offences Against Property) and Tort Law*, in this series. The test is therefore whether it was reasonably foreseeable that the victim would be injured.

However, the more recent case of *R* v *Singh* (1999) established the current rule whereby 'the circumstances must be such that a reasonably prudent person would have foreseen a serious and obvious risk not merely of injury or even of serious injury but of death'. In this case, the victim was a tenant who died of carbon monoxide poisoning and his death was foreseeable by the landlord's son, who was in charge of maintaining the tenant's property. In *R* v *Misra and Srivastava* (2004), two doctors were convicted of gross negligence manslaughter after a patient died from toxic-shock syndrome (where a simple course of antibiotics would have saved his life), and the Court of Appeal confirmed this test — that the risk to which the victim must be exposed is a risk of death. In *Brown* v *R* (2005), the Privy Council even suggested that only a very high risk of death would suffice.

Professor J. C. Smith commented: 'It seems that the deliberate taking of a high degree of risk of causing serious bodily harm which results in death (formerly murder under *Hyam* v *DPP*) must now be manslaughter.' This decision clarifies one of the major problems with the speech of Lord Mackay LC in *R* v *Adomako,* by requiring a risk in respect of which the defendant was negligent to have been one of death rather than any lesser degree of harm. If, however, a defendant is reckless as to a lesser degree of harm but does cause a victim's death, this may amount to reckless manslaughter — a category of manslaughter that Lord Mackay left open (but which forms the focus of considerable academic speculation, although not featuring in the law reports).

Examples of situations where a duty of care is owed are doctor–patient and landlord–tenant relationships. In the unreported case of *R* v *Becker*, the defendant, a doctor on an emergency call, attended a patient at home. The patient was suffering from a kidney stone and, having made a correct diagnosis, the doctor prescribed a painkiller. As the painkiller did not work fast enough, the doctor decided to prescribe an opiate as well. Although the patient indicated that the pain had now eased, the doctor went ahead with the injection of 30mg of diamorphine and the patient died later that day from the overdose. The doctor was convicted of manslaughter by gross negligence after a trial in which it was common ground that the injection of that quantity of the drug (about three times the largest permissible dose) was conduct falling below the standard expected of a reasonably competent GP. The sole issue for the jury had been whether that amounted to gross negligence. This conviction was then upheld by the Court of Appeal.

It would appear from cases such as *R* v *Khan* (1998) and *Lewin* v *CPS* (2002) that judges are reluctant to extend the areas in which there could be a duty of care. The *Khan* case involved a pimp who gave heroin to a prostitute and then left her, even when it was clear that she was in a coma, from which she died. In *Lewin*, the defendant, a friend of the victim, left him in a car after a heavy drinking session in Marbella.

Breach of duty of care
The test for what constitutes a breach of the duty of care causing the death of the victim is again the tort test. The defendant's conduct must have gone below the standard to be expected of a reasonable person. This then requires the various 'risk' factors to be considered, for example probability of harm and seriousness of injury. Note the second part of the rule for gross negligence manslaughter, that the breach must have caused death. To judge whether it has done so, the legal rules of causation need to be considered, and also the factual 'but for' test, where the question is asked: but for the defendant's action, would the defendant still be alive?

Gross negligence
Gross negligence is the *mens rea* for the offence and, as can be seen from Lord Hewart CJ's statement in *R* v *Bateman* (above), this is a question for the jury to decide. It must consider whether, having regard to the risk of death involved, the conduct of the

defendant was so bad in all the circumstances as to amount in its judgement to a criminal act or omission.

In *R* v *Adomako*, Lord Taylor CJ indicated that gross negligence could include the following:
- indifference to an obvious risk of injury to health
- actual foresight of the risk, coupled with the determination nevertheless to run it
- an appreciation of the risk, coupled with an intention to avoid it but also coupled with such a high degree of negligence in the attempted avoidance as the jury considers conviction justified
- inattention or failure to address a serious risk that went beyond 'mere inadvertence' in respect of an obvious and important matter that the defendant's duty demanded he should address

In this case, the defendant was an anaesthetist who, during an eye operation, failed to notice that the patient's breathing tube had become disconnected. In the 4 minutes between the disconnection and the alarm sounding on the machine monitoring the patient's blood pressure, the defendant also failed to notice that the patient was turning blue through anoxia, the dials on the mechanical ventilating machine were not operating and the alarm on the ventilator was not switched on. An expert witness stated that these problems would have been obvious to any competent anaesthetist within 15 seconds. The case was appealed to the House of Lords, with the result that this branch of the law returned to the traditional rules laid down in *R* v *Bateman* and *Andrews* v *DPP* (1937) after a 'wrong turn' had been taken in both *R* v *Lawrence* (1981) and *R* v *Seymour* (1983).

Reckless manslaughter

Following *R* v *Adomako*, it was believed that the category of reckless manslaughter no longer existed but had been 'absorbed' by gross negligence manslaughter. However, in *R* v *Lidar* (1999), the Court of Appeal developed the current test for this type of involuntary manslaughter. The test is whether the defendant was aware of a risk of death or serious injury and nonetheless proceeded unreasonably to take that risk — provided that his or her action was the cause of death. That test is, of course, subjective. In the *Lidar* case, the defendant was the driver of a moving car onto which the victim was clinging while fighting the defendant. The victim fell and was killed when the car ran him over. The appeal court held that the trial judge was correct in his view that this was a case of reckless manslaughter and right in directing the jury accordingly.

As Janet Loveless writes in *Complete Criminal Law: Test, Cases, and Materials*:

> The main difficulty here is to distinguish recklessness from oblique intention. If you think back to *Hyam*, for instance, in pouring paraffin through a letterbox and igniting it, the defendant foresaw a highly probable risk of death/GBH but no certainty. The court considered that such foresight was sufficient *mens rea* for murder...Now Mrs Hyam would be considered subjectively reckless and guilty of either reckless or unlawful and dangerous act manslaughter but not murder.

Defences

In this unit, candidates are usually required to consider defences that may be available to the defendant, in addition to explaining the *actus reus* and *mens rea* of the appropriate offence. Students need to learn these defences and to be able to apply them in problem-solving questions.

Consent

Like the defence of intoxication, consent has limited and controlled applications. Indeed, the general rule is that it is *not* a defence where non-fatal crimes are concerned. In *Attorney General's Reference (No. 6 of 1980)*, the Court of Appeal decided that where two people fight, the blows inflicted can amount to battery, and that the unlawfulness cannot be denied by one party pleading that the other consented to the fight. Lord Lane CJ stated:

> It is not in the public interest that people should try to cause each other bodily harm for no good reason. Minor struggles are another matter. So, in our judgement, it is immaterial whether the act occurs in private or in public; it is an assault if actual bodily harm is intended and/or caused. This means that most fights will be unlawful regardless of consent.

This confirms the view taken by Swift J in *R v Donovan* (1934), where he stated: 'It is an unlawful act to beat another person with such a degree of violence that the infliction of bodily harm is a probable consequence, and when such an act is proved, consent is immaterial.'

The first rule to be established if consent is to be pleaded successfully is that the alleged victim's consent must not have been obtained by deception or, if it was, then the deception must not have been such as to alter his or her perception of the nature and quality of the act complained of. In *R v Richardson* (1999), the defendant was a registered dentist who had been suspended from practice by the General Dental Council. While suspended, she had carried out dentistry on a number of patients, and the mother of two of these patients complained to the police. A prosecution was brought for actual bodily harm (ABH) and the defendant was convicted. On appeal she argued that the complainant had consented to the treatment. The appeal was allowed because there had been no deception as to the nature and quality of the dental work; if there had been, it would have cancelled out the consent.

A potentially broader interpretation of this question of consent was taken in *R v Tabassum* (2000), where it was held that a mistake as to the medical qualifications of the defendant meant that the victim did not know the quality of the act the defendant carried out and therefore could not have consented to it.

The next general rule is that consent may only be pleaded to the crimes of assault and battery and not to any more serious crime, unless the circumstances fall under the following heads:

- Sporting activities such as football, rugby and hockey, where physical contact is effectively part of the sport. In these cases, players are deemed to have consented to even serious injuries, provided these occurred when the players were acting within the rules of the game; see *R v Billinghurst* (1978). However, in *R v Barnes* (2004), Lord Woolf CJ ruled that:

  > ...In highly competitive sports, where conduct outside the rules could be expected to occur in the heat of the moment, such conduct might not reach the threshold level required for it to be criminal. That level was an objective one which would be determined by the type of sport, the level at which it was played...the degree of force used, the extent of the risk of injury and the state of mind of the accused.

- Rough horseplay. In *R v Jones* (1987), a gang of schoolboys threw their victims up to 3 metres into the air, with the result that one victim suffered a ruptured spleen and broke his arm on hitting the floor. The defence was allowed on the basis that there was no intention to cause injury, and on appeal, convictions for grievous bodily harm (GBH) were quashed. Another case to illustrate this exception is *R v Richardson and Irwin* (1999). The two defendants, their victim and others were university students who had been out drinking. On returning to their accommodation, they indulged in horseplay as on previous occasions. This culminated in the victim being lifted over the edge of a balcony, from which he was dropped and fell about 3 metres. He suffered serious injuries and both defendants were charged with and convicted of a s.20 offence. The Court of Appeal quashed their convictions because the trial judge had confused subjective and objective recklessness in his direction to the jury. More importantly, the court held that, where a defendant pleads voluntary intoxication in response to an offence of basic intent, the Crown must prove that the defendant would have foreseen the risk, had he or she not been intoxicated. It was also held that a mistaken belief by a defendant that his or her victim was consenting to run the risk of personal injury would enable the defendant to avoid liability, even if that mistake was induced by intoxication.

- Surgery, including tattooing and body piercing. In *R v Wilson* (1996), the defendant had, at his wife's request, used a hot knife to brand his initials onto her bottom. The scars were found during a medical examination and he was subsequently charged with s.47 ABH. At his trial, it was argued that his wife had consented to his conduct, but the judge ruled (following *R v Brown*, a 1994 case involving sadomasochism) that this defence was not available on these facts. However, his appeal was allowed on the basis that it fell within the exception of tattooing recognised by *R v Brown*, from which case it was distinguished on the ground that Mrs Wilson had not only consented to the branding but had actually instigated it, and there was clearly no aggressive intent on the part of the husband. The court finally ruled per Russell LJ that 'consensual activity between husband and wife, in the privacy of the matrimonial home, is not, in our judgement, normally a proper matter for criminal investigation, let alone criminal prosecution'.

Insanity

The legal rules governing decisions about the criminal liability of insane people are known as the **M'Naghten rules**. These state that:

> To establish a defence on the ground of insanity, it must be clearly proved that, at the time of the committing of the act, the party accused was labouring under such a defect of reason, from disease of the mind, as not to know the nature and quality of the act he was doing, or, if he did know it, that he did not know he was doing what was wrong.

As with the partial defence of diminished responsibility, the burden of proof rests on the defendant and the standard of proof is the balance of probability.

To sum up, a defendant must be acquitted:
- if, because of a disease of the mind, he or she did not know the nature and quality of his or her act
- if, because of a disease of the mind, he or she did not know his or her act was wrong, even if he or she did know the nature and quality of his or her act

After the introduction of the partial defence of diminished responsibility under s.2 of the **Homicide Act 1957**, this defence was rarely used. However, in the 5 years since the introduction of the **Criminal Procedure (Insanity) Act 1991**, there were 44 findings of 'not guilty by reason of insanity'. Michael Allen in *Elliott and Wood's Cases and Materials on Criminal Law* suggests that this increase in the use of insanity as a defence can be attributed to 'an appreciation that the 1991 Act has removed the more glaring disincentives inherent within the 1964 Criminal Procedure (Insanity) Act'.

Smith and Hogan Criminal Law states:

> When a defendant puts his state of mind in issue, the question of whether he has raised the defence of insanity is one of law for the judge. Whether a defendant, or indeed his medical witnesses, would call the condition on which he relies 'insanity' is immaterial. The expert witnesses may testify as to the factual nature of the condition but it is for the judge to say whether that is evidence of a 'defect of reason from disease of the mind' because these are legal, not medical concepts.

Disease of the mind

Any disease that produces a mental malfunctioning is a disease of the mind. Physical conditions such as arteriosclerosis, brain tumours, epilepsy and diabetes may all amount in law to diseases of the mind if they produce the relevant malfunction. A malfunctioning of the mind is *not* a disease of the mind when it is brought about by some external factor, for example a blow on the head causing concussion or the consumption of alcohol or drugs. In *Bratty* v *Attorney General for Northern Ireland* (1963), Lord Denning MR defined a disease of the mind as follows: 'It seems to me that any mental disorder which has manifested itself in violence and is prone to recur is a disease of the mind.'

In *R* v *Kemp* (1957), the defendant, who was suffering from arteriosclerosis, made a savage attack on his wife with a hammer. It was argued that his defect of reason arose from a purely physical condition and not from any mental disease. It was further contended that, if a physical disease caused the brain cells to degenerate, then it would be a disease of the mind, but, until it did so, it was a temporary interference with the working of the brain that was not unlike concussion and was not a disease of the mind. Devlin J rejected this argument and ruled that the defendant was suffering from a disease of the mind:

> The law is not concerned with the brain but with the mind, in the sense that 'mind' is ordinarily used, the mental faculties of reason, memory and understanding...In my judgement the condition of the brain is irrelevant and so is the question of whether the condition of the mind is curable or incurable, transitory or permanent.

Defect of reason

The basis of the M'Naghten rules is that the disease of the mind must have given rise to a defect of reason. This means that the defendant's powers of reasoning must have been impaired; a mere failure to use the powers of reasoning that one has is not within the rules. See *R v Clarke* (1972), where the defendant claimed she had taken articles from a supermarket without paying for them because of absentmindedness resulting from depression. It was held that, even if she was suffering from a disease of the mind, she had not raised the defence of insanity but was simply denying that she had *mens rea*.

Not knowing the nature and quality of the act

The ignorance referred to here is ignorance of the physical, rather than the moral, nature of the act, for example where a man cuts a woman's throat, believing he is cutting a loaf of bread, or where a nurse throws a baby into a fire thinking it is a log. People who kill under the influence of delusions such as these cannot be convicted of murder as they lack the required *mens rea*.

Not knowing the act is wrong

It is established law that this requirement means legally and not morally wrong. Even if the defendant did not know that his or her action was against the law, he or she is still liable if he or she knew it was wrong 'according to the ordinary standard adopted by reasonable men'.

In *R v Windle* (1952), the defendant killed his wife, who was certifiably insane and always speaking of committing suicide. He then telephoned the police and, when he was arrested, said: 'I suppose they will hang me for this.' At his trial, the defence of insanity was not allowed to go to the jury, since the words he used indicated that he knew killing his wife was legally wrong. Research by Mackay, Mitchell and Howe, published in the *Criminal Law Review*, suggests that psychiatrists have extended this limb of the defence to include situations where, although the defendant recognised his or her actions were unlawful, he or she thought they were morally justified.

Automatism

Automatism is recognised as a defence to all crimes. It refers to the situation where the defendant's actions are involuntary, in the sense that they are beyond his or her control. Typical examples are reflex actions and acts committed while sleepwalking or undergoing a hypnotic trance or convulsions.

The rationale for this defence is clear. The defendant in such a situation is not responsible for the consequences of his or her actions. The act is, in a sense, not his or her own. He or she does not deserve to be punished, nor would punishment serve any useful or rational purpose.

Although automatism has been referred to as a 'defence', the legally accurate analysis is that voluntariness is a basic ingredient of criminal liability. The onus, therefore, is on the prosecution to prove beyond reasonable doubt that the conduct of the defendant was willed. Note, however, that the prosecution is obliged to prove that the acts of the defendant were voluntary only if the defendant has introduced evidence (generally of a medical type) that he or she was an automaton at the relevant time.

A good hypothetical example of automatism (a driver losing control of his car as he instinctively tries to fend off a swarm of bees that entered through an open window) was given by the judge in *Hill* v *Baxter* (1958). The response to this kind of stimulus is an automatic one, a reflex response, and it is easy to sustain the argument that the defendant should not be held liable for the consequences resulting from loss of control of his vehicle.

Lord Denning MR in *Bratty* v *Attorney General for Northern Ireland* stated:

> The requirement that it should be a voluntary act is essential...in every criminal case. No act is punishable if it is done involuntarily; and an involuntary act in this context — some people...prefer to speak of it as 'automatism' — means an act which is done by the muscles without any control by the mind, such as a spasm, a reflex action or a convulsion; or an act done by a person who is not conscious of what he is doing, such as an act done whilst suffering from concussion or whilst sleepwalking.

He went on to stress that an act is not to be regarded as involuntary if the person was conscious but nevertheless could not control his or her actions (irresistible impulse) or could not remember after the event exactly what took place.

In *Broome* v *Perkins* (1987), the defendant was charged with driving without due care and attention. He had driven erratically for 6 miles. It was held that even though there was some evidence to establish that he was suffering from hypoglycaemia (low blood sugar), he must have been exercising conscious control of the vehicle, even though imperfectly, in order to have manoeuvred it reasonably successfully over such a distance. See also *Attorney General's Reference (No. 2 of 1992)*, where the defence of 'partial awareness' was disallowed by the Court of Appeal.

Both these cases emphasised the need for total loss of control, although the Law Commission's Draft Criminal Code of 1989, as yet not incorporated into law, has suggested that effective loss of control would suffice. Also note that where defendants were, or became, aware that they might lose conscious control of their actions, then the defence is likely to be rejected.

Insane automatism

If the automatism results from a 'disease of the mind' under the M'Naghten rules, the condition amounts to what in law is known as insanity. In such circumstances, the defendant is entitled to no more than a qualified acquittal by the special verdict of 'not guilty by reason of insanity'. In such a case, the judge must make one of various orders under the **Criminal Procedure (Insanity and Unfitness to Plead) Act 1991**.

In *Bratty*, it was held, following *R v Kemp* (the arteriosclerosis case), that if the defendant leads evidence of automatism, the prosecution is allowed to lead evidence that the condition giving rise to the automatism is a 'disease of the mind' and the defendant is entitled only to a qualified acquittal. If the trial judge concludes, on the evidence, that the condition is a disease of the mind, he or she is entitled to refuse to let the defence of non-insane automatism go to the jury. In those circumstances, he or she is obliged to instruct the jury that insanity is the only defence available to the defendant.

For a defendant to have what amounts to a 'disease of the mind', it does not matter whether the cause of the mental impairment is organic (as in epilepsy) or functional (as in schizophrenia). Nor does it matter whether the impairment is permanent or transient and intermittent, provided that it was operative at the time of the alleged offence (see the 1984 case of *R v Sullivan*). In *Bratty*, Lord Denning MR said that any condition that has 'manifested itself in violence and is prone to recur is a disease of the mind'. This reflects what many regard as the central policy underlying the insanity defence: to control those who, although not criminally responsible for the harm caused, are perceived to be suffering from a condition that makes them 'dangerous'.

Non-insane automatism

This defence may apply where the automatism is induced by an external factor such as a blow to the head causing concussion or a reflex spasm (as in the example given in *Hill v Baxter*). This gives rise to criticism when acts committed by someone sleepwalking or undergoing an epileptic episode fail to be considered as acts of insane automatism. The law on automatism as it affects diabetics has been the subject of particular criticism because, depending on whether the diabetic's diagnosis is hypoglycaemia (low blood sugar) or hyperglycaemia (high blood sugar), the appropriate defence is judged to be non-insane or insane automatism respectively. In *R v Quick* (1973), a defendant who took his insulin but failed to eat was able to plead non-insane automatism, but in *R v Hennessy* (1989), a defendant who had failed to take sufficient insulin was held to have a defence of insane automatism (which, incidentally, caused him to change his plea to guilty rather than face indefinite detention in a mental hospital).

In *R v T* (1990), the application of the internal/external factor test led to a just decision. The defendant, who suffered from post-traumatic stress disorder as a consequence of being raped, stabbed someone during a robbery. The trial judge ruled that the stress had been caused by the external factor of the rape and accordingly the defence was that of non-insane automatism. Note that where a defendant's automatism has been caused by the consumption of alcohol or dangerous drugs, the defence becomes intoxication.

Self-defence

Where an attack of a violent, unlawful or indecent nature is made so that the victim fears for his or her life or safety, then he or she is entitled to protect himself or herself and to repel such attack by force, provided that he or she uses no more force than is reasonable in the circumstances; see Lord Morris's comments in *Palmer* v *R* (1971).

There is a common law right of self-defence. In addition, s.3(1) of the **Criminal Law Act 1967** states: 'A person may use such force as is reasonable in the circumstances in the prevention of crime, or in effecting or assisting in the lawful arrest of offenders or suspected offenders or of persons unlawfully at large.' Where justified, self-defence can provide a complete defence to charges of murder or any non-fatal offence against the person; the defence operates by negating the unlawfulness of the homicide or assault.

The first requirement (as stated by Janet Loveless in *Complete Criminal Law: Test, Cases, and Materials*, is that 'defensive force will only be lawful if it is necessary, and it will only be necessary if it used to resist, repel or ward off an unjust imminent threat. The act of self-defence cannot be retaliatory or revengeful'. An attack at some future point will not be sufficiently imminent — this means 'fairly immediate'.

The second requirement is that the degree of force must be reasonable. Factors that may be taken into account in determining what is reasonable force for the purpose of both common-law and statutory defences are:
- the nature and degree of force used
- the gravity of the crime or evil to be prevented
- the relative strength of the parties concerned and the number of people involved

The law does not require proportionate force, but the degree of force must be capable of being seen as only so much as is necessary to repel an attack. Excessive force will usually be evidence that the attack was retaliatory and therefore not in self-defence; see *R* v *Martin* (2002).

To reject self-defence as a defence, the jury must be satisfied that no reasonable person, put in the defendant's position and with the time for reflection that the defendant had, would consider the violence he or she used to be justifiable; see *Farrell* v *Secretary of State for Defence* (1980). Thus, objectivity is tempered with the personal situation of the actual defendant. The test is whether or not the defendant used reasonable force in the agony of the situation, and not whether the force used would be considered reasonable by the defendant or a reasonable person, viewing the situation in cool isolation.

Further points to consider
- Where the defendant has used excessive (and therefore unreasonable) force, neither the common law nor the statutory defence of self-defence will be open to him or her, and his or her criminal liability will be determined by his or her *mens rea* and the harm he or she has inflicted.

- The law has no sympathy with drunkenness, so that an honest mistake made by a drunken defendant will render the defence of self-defence inadmissible; see *R v O'Grady* (1987).
- As to the duty of a defendant to retreat before acting in self-defence, the case of *R v Bird* (1985) held that proof that the defendant in this case had tried to retreat was a method of rebutting the suggestion that she was an attacker, but was not the only method.
- It also appears from *Attorney General's Reference (No. 2 of 1983)* that, in certain circumstances, a person is not obliged to wait until he or she is attacked before taking steps towards self-protection.
- The lawful use of self-defence is limited when it comes to protecting property. Professor Andrew Ashworth comments in *Principles of Criminal Law*:

> What is crucial is that it should rule out the infliction or risk of considerable physical harm merely to apprehend a fleeing thief, to stop minor property loss or damage...The proper approach is to compare the relative value of the rights involved, and not to give special weight to the rights of the property owner simply because the other party is in the wrong (i.e. committing a crime).

Mistake

In most cases of mistake, the defendant will argue that his or her mistake negates the *mens rea* required for the crime in question. It is clearly established that, for the defence to succeed, the mistake must be one of fact and not of law. In *R v Reid* (1973), a driver refused to take a breath test because he mistakenly believed the policeman had no right to require him to do so. The defence of mistake was disallowed on the ground that ignorance of law cannot amount to a mistake.

In cases where defendants have defended themselves because they honestly but mistakenly believed themselves to be under attack, the defence of self-defence must be judged according to the mistaken view of the facts, regardless of whether the mistake was reasonable or not. In *R v Williams* (1984), a passer-by called Mason saw a youth rob a woman. He chased and caught the youth and knocked him to the ground. He then told another passer-by, the appellant, Williams, that he was a police officer (which was untrue) and that he was arresting the youth. Williams asked to see Mason's warrant card and, when this was not produced, a struggle ensued during which Williams punched Mason in the face. In his defence, Williams claimed that he honestly believed that the youth was being unlawfully assaulted by Mason and that he was trying to rescue him. He was convicted of ABH under s.47, following a direction to the jury that his mistake would be relevant only if it was honest and based on reasonable grounds.

On appeal, Lord Lane CJ stated:

> The reasonableness or unreasonableness of the defendant's belief is material to the question of whether the belief was held by the defendant at all. If the belief was in fact held, its unreasonableness, so far as guilt or innocence is concerned, is neither here nor there. It is irrelevant... The jury should be directed first of all that the prosecution have the burden of

proving the unlawfulness of the defendant's actions; secondly, if the defendant may have been labouring under a mistake as to the facts, he must be judged according to his mistaken view of the facts; thirdly, that is so whether the mistake was, on an objective view, a reasonable mistake or not... Even if the jury come to the conclusion that the mistake was an unreasonable one, if the defendant may genuinely have been labouring under it, he is entitled to rely on it.

The Judicial Studies Board has produced a model direction on self-defence (see **www.jsboard.co.uk**), which states:

Whether the plea is self-defence or defence of another, if the defendant may have been honestly mistaken as to the facts, he must be judged according to his mistaken view of the facts: that is so whether the mistake was, on an objective view, a reasonable mistake or not.

Intoxication

Students often find the defence of intoxication difficult to deal with because the way in which it operates, if at all, depends on variables in terms of types of intoxication — whether voluntary or involuntary, whether by alcohol or illegal drugs or by sedative or prescribed drugs — and on whether or not the particular offence charged is an offence of basic or specific intent.

The first general rule to learn is that, as *Smith and Hogan Criminal Law* states:

Intoxication is not, and never has been, a defence in itself. It is never a defence for a defendant to say, however convincingly, that but for the drink he would not have behaved as he did. Because alcohol and other drugs weaken the restraints and inhibitions which normally govern our conduct, a man may do things when drunk that he would never dream of doing while sober. If, however, he had the *mens rea* for the crime charged he is guilty, even though drink impaired or negatived his ability to judge between right and wrong or to resist temptation or provocation and even though, in his drunken state, he found the impulse to act as he did irresistible.

Voluntary intoxication by alcohol or illegal drugs

The legal rule is that voluntary intoxication by alcohol or illegal drugs is at best a partial defence for anyone charged with offences of specific intent such as murder and s.18 GBH with intent. For basic intent offences, it will be rejected. In the leading case of *DPP v Beard* (1920), it was held that if a defendant charged with murder can prove that, at the time of committing the crime, he or she was so drunk as to be unable to form the necessary *mens rea* of intent for the crime, he or she will be acquitted of that offence but convicted of the basic-intent offence — so that the verdict will not be murder but manslaughter, and, in other cases, not s.18 GBH but s.20. However, the courts have relaxed this rule somewhat, on the basis that it would not be fair to require the defendant to prove his or her incapacity. The test now is whether the defendant's intoxication negated his or her specific intent because it prevented him or her from foreseeing the prohibited consequence. In *DPP v Majewski* (1977), this approach was confirmed. Here the defendant was charged with the assault of a policeman — an offence of basic intent — and his defence of drunkenness was rejected.

As for intoxication by illegal drugs, the same applies. In *R v Lipman* (1970), the defendant, having taken a quantity of LSD and believing as a result that he was being attacked by snakes in the centre of the earth, attacked and killed his girlfriend, cramming a sheet into her mouth. At his trial, he was acquitted of murder, but his plea of intoxication was not accepted as a defence to manslaughter. The Court of Appeal stated that when a killing results from an unlawful act of the defendant, no specific intent has to be proved to convict of manslaughter. Self-induced intoxication is no defence, and since the acts complained of were obviously likely to harm the victim, the verdict of manslaughter was inevitable.

Voluntary intoxication using sedative drugs

If a defendant has taken drugs that normally have a sedative or soporific effect, making the user relaxed or sleepy, he or she is usually treated as being involuntarily intoxicated. In *R v Hardie* (1985), the defendant, after taking Valium tablets prescribed for the woman with whom he shared a flat, started a fire when she asked him to leave, and he was charged and convicted under the **Criminal Damage Act 1971**. The Court of Appeal, quashing this conviction, overturned the trial judge's direction to the jury, which had made no mention of the distinction the law draws between dangerous/illegal and prescription/sedative drugs. The court also indicated that, in this case, the jury should have been invited to consider whether the defendant's taking of six Valium tablets was objectively reckless; following *R v G* (2003), the test would now be one of subjective recklessness.

Involuntary intoxication

Involuntary intoxication refers to the situation where defendants claim that they did not know they were taking alcohol or an intoxicating drug because their food or drink was laced without their knowledge. The legal rule here is that, if this negates the *mens rea* of the offence, it will be a full defence to any type of offence, whether one of specific or basic intent.

However, in the difficult case of *R v Kingston* (1994), which involved a defendant who was attracted to young boys, the defendant was drugged without his knowledge by his co-defendant, who had intended to blackmail him. His defence to a charge of indecent assault was that the involuntary intoxication effectively disinhibited him, and that, if sober, he would not have carried out these acts. The Court of Appeal allowed his appeal, holding that if a surreptitiously administered drug causes a person to lose his self-control and so form an intent he would not otherwise have formed, the law should not hold him or her liable, as the operative fault is not his or hers. This novel argument was rejected by the House of Lords, which approved the trial judge's direction to the jury that an intoxicated intent was still intent, and the fact that the intoxication was involuntary made no difference.

Intoxication causing insanity or abnormality of mind

It is settled law that, where excessively heavy drinking causes actual insanity, such as the condition of *delirium tremens*, then the M'Naghten rules apply and the defence becomes one of insanity. As regards the issue of abnormality of mind giving rise to the possible (partial) defence to murder of diminished responsibility under s.2 of the **Homicide Act 1956**, it is also clear that self-induced intoxication must be ignored in deciding whether the defendant was suffering from such an abnormality of mind as to amount to diminished responsibility; exceptions to this arise if it can be proved that the defendant suffered from alcohol dependency syndrome, which caused an abnormality of mind, or that the craving for drink or drugs was itself an abnormality of mind; see *R Wood* (2008) and *R* v *Dietschmann* (2003), pp. 13–14.

Critical evaluation of law on offences against the person

In this examination paper, Question 3 is always about how well you can evaluate or criticise a particular area of law, for example homicide in general, murder or involuntary manslaughter as separate offences, and non-fatal offences.

To help you succeed in dealing with this kind of question, this section includes specific material on some of these issues.

The major weaknesses of past candidates are as follows.
- Giving answers that largely repeat the rules of the issue of law that they have already explained or applied in answer to an earlier question. Some marks will be awarded for this kind of answer, but never high marks, because such candidates have not answered the question set.
- Failing to produce a well-explained analysis of weaknesses in the law, plus consideration of what aspects of that law are broadly satisfactory, and then a reasoned conclusion.
- Lack of planning. All law questions — and the critical evaluation questions in particular — demand a level of pre-planning. You must leave ample time for this aspect of the answer otherwise you will almost certainly fall into the traps outlined above. Write 'spider diagrams' or some other form of outline of your answer, in terms of both content and structure.
- Poor time planning. The critical evaluation questions comprise a third of the overall marks for this paper and must therefore be given at least a third of the time allocation.
- Failing to explain what improvements or reforms could be made to the law, whether the question explicitly asks for this or not. Ideally, this will be a summary of Law Commission recommendations, but do not be afraid to include your own ideas, especially if these are based on topical debates.

Critical evaluation of the law on non-fatal offences

Terminology
First, it may be said that the non-fatal offences are badly defined. There are still no clear statutory definitions of assault and battery, while the definitions of the more serious

offences are contained in an Act passed well over 100 years ago. The Act has been described as 'a rag-bag of offences brought together from a wide variety of sources with no attempt, as the draftsman frankly acknowledged, to introduce consistency as to substance or as to form'. Much of the vocabulary, such as 'assault' in s.47 and 'maliciously' in s.18, is antiquated and even misleading. In s.18, the word 'maliciously' means nothing in its primary use because the *mens rea* is already defined as 'with intent', whereas in s.20 the same word means recklessness or basic intent as to inflicting some harm. The word 'wounding' again has a technical rather than common definition. Although the Joint Charging Standard, agreed by the police and the Crown Prosecution Service, substantially clarifies the issue of what charge to bring for different levels of injury, nonetheless any injury that causes blood to flow, even a grazed knee or a minor cut, could potentially be charged as wounding.

Another linguistic criticism concerns the use of 'inflict' in s.20 and 'cause' in s.18 of the **Offences Against the Person Act 1861**. It is argued that the word 'inflict' requires a battery to take place for the full offence to be committed, and this was the central issue raised in the case of *R* v *Burstow* (1997), decided by the House of Lords. The Court of Appeal in that case had certified the question: 'Whether an offence of inflicting grievous bodily harm under s.20 can be committed where no physical violence is applied directly or indirectly.' It was argued that it is inherent in the word 'inflict' that there must be some application of force to the body, but in the earlier case of *R* v *Wilson* (1984), Lord Roskill was 'content to accept that there can be the infliction of GBH contrary to s.20 without an assault (battery) being committed'. Lord Steyn, in the leading judgement in *R* v *Burstow*, ruled that 'there is no radical difference between the meaning of the words "cause" and "inflict"'. Lord Hope went even further when he stated that 'for all practical purposes there is, in my opinion, no difference between these two words'. In a later section he continued: 'In the context of a criminal act, therefore, the words "cause" and "inflict" may be take to be interchangeable.' This question, however, was the main defence issue in the 2005 case of *R* v *Dica*, which concerned biological GBH.

Students need to be aware of the secondary *mens rea* for a s.18 offence — 'intention to resist or prevent the lawful apprehension of any person'. Although it was stated in *R* v *Mowatt* (1968) that the word 'malicious' means nothing, *Smith and Hogan Criminal Law* submits that, as regards this particular section, the prosecution needs to be able to prove that a defendant in seeking to avoid arrest must at least have been reckless as to causing some harm. Nevertheless, it is obvious that the respective *mens rea* elements for a s.18 offence are significantly unbalanced.

Sentencing

The hierarchy of the non-fatal offences according to seriousness can also be severely criticised. While the maximum punishment for assault and battery is 6 months' imprisonment, an ABH offence under s.47 of the **Offences Against the Person Act 1861** receives a custodial sentence of up to 5 years. Yet the only real difference between the offences is the ABH caused in a s.47 offence — and ABH can mean as little as causing discomfort to the person. In addition, the s.20 offence is defined as much more serious than a s.47 one as regards both its *actus reus* and its *mens rea*, and yet they share the same maximum sentence. It is accepted judicial practice in sentencing that the maximum sentence will rarely be imposed and then only for the most severe type of offence, but the fact remains that the maximum sentences for s.47 and s.20 offences are identical, and it is manifestly unfair that this should be the case when both the *actus reus* and the *mens rea* required for a s.20 conviction are much greater than those for s.47.

A further problem is that the only significant difference between s.20 and s.18 is arguably a slightly more serious *mens rea* under s.18, yet the maximum sentence leaps from 5 years for s.20 to life for s.18. This can perhaps be justified by the fact that a defendant who intends to cause GBH within s.18 has the *mens rea* of murder, and it is merely chance that dictates whether the victim of a stabbing survives or dies. It should be noted that only 23% of offenders indicted under s.18 are eventually convicted of that offence, with most of the remainder being convicted of (or having the charge reduced to) lesser offences of violence such as s.20. While there are many reasons for this, one clear reason is the difficulty of proving the required specific intention for s.18.

Constructive intent

The third and possibly most serious criticism that can be directed against the present law is the issue of constructive intent seen in both s.47 and s.20 offences, where the defendant is made liable to a possible 5-year sentence, more because of the outcome — which will, in many cases, have been unforeseen and unintended — than because of the degree of *mens rea*. This runs counter to the basic requirement of criminal liability — that it should depend on, and indeed reflect, the amount of fault, i.e. *mens rea*, possessed by the defendant.

Development of statutory offences through case law

The final argument concerning the present state of the law on non-fatal offences must surely be about the ways in which the statutory offences in the **Offences Against the Person Act 1861** are almost constantly being redefined through reported cases. It is unsatisfactory for so many changes to be made to statutory offences by means of case law, which by its nature can be amended by later cases being appealed to the Court of Appeal or the House of Lords. This is both an unnecessary and expensive appeals process, arising from wrong decisions on questions of law. The cases of *R v Ireland* and *R v Burstow* in 1998 have considerably extended the law on assault and s.20 GBH, and *R v Dica* (2005) seems to have created a further major extension to the definition of GBH. In the *Dica* case, the defendant was convicted of causing 'biological' GBH when he tricked two women into having unprotected sexual intercourse with him, even though he had been diagnosed with HIV in 1995. This follows the conviction in Scotland of Stephen Kelly in 2001 of 'reckless conduct' after passing HIV to his wife.

In the Court of Appeal, Dica's conviction was quashed and a retrial was ordered to consider the defence argument of consent. Meanwhile the court ruled that injury by reckless infection in the course of sexual activity does fall within the scope of s.20 of the **Offences Against the Person Act** — unless the alleged victim consents to run the risk. This decision clearly overruled the case of *R v Clarence* (1889), where a husband was prosecuted for infecting his unsuspecting wife with gonorrhoea but his conviction was quashed by a House of Lords ruling that s.20 required an assault or some form of direct bodily violence. In the *New Law Journal* of 21 May 2004, J. R. Spencer QC wrote that the court:

> ...condemned [*R v Clarence*] as inconsistent with later cases, notably *R v Ireland*; *R v Burstow*, which hold that s.20 covers deliberate harassment leading to psychiatric injury... If psychiatric injury can be inflicted without direct or indirect violence or an assault, for the purposes of s.20 physical injury may be similarly inflicted.

Even more importantly, the Court of Appeal has apparently widened the scope of the defence of consent in such cases, distinguishing the case of *R v Brown* (1994), where this defence was expressly disallowed by the House of Lords. Here, the court ruled that 'there is a vital difference between consenting to the deliberate infliction of harm, and consenting to an activity that you know involves a risk of it'. This ruling means that criminal liability does not arise where the other party, knows, or suspects, and is prepared to take the risk.

Proposed law reform

The draft Criminal Law Bill, issued by the Home Office in 1998, based on the Law Commission's recommendations of 5 years earlier and not yet enacted as law, proposes to update the language used for these offences by talking about 'serious injury' rather than 'grievous bodily harm', and avoiding the words 'maliciously' and 'wounding' altogether. Under the bill, s.18 would be replaced by 'intentionally causing serious injury' (for which the maximum penalty would be life imprisonment); s.20 by 'recklessly causing serious injury' (maximum penalty 7 years); and s.47 by 'intentionally or recklessly causing injury' (maximum penalty 5 years). The bill still uses the term 'assault' for the two separate offences of assault and battery.

The preamble of the Home Office's consultation paper, 'Violence: Reforming the Offences Against the Person Act 1861', states:

> It is...particularly important that the law governing such behaviour should be robust, clear and well understood. Unclear or uncertain criminal law risks creating injustice and unfairness to individuals, as well as making the work of the police and courts far more difficult and time-consuming.

It is, therefore, to be regretted that, 11 years after these words were written and 16 years after the Law Commission published its recommendations for reform, these reforms have still not been the subject of legislation.

Critical evaluation of the law on fatal offences

Murder

When the Law Commission's 2006 report on murder, manslaughter and infanticide declared 'The law governing homicide in England and Wales is a rickety structure set upon shaky foundations', it was stating what many practising and academic lawyers had been arguing for years.

Lack of a code

The first severe criticism is that the law on murder is common law, made and developed by judges through reported cases. In all other developed countries, including other common law countries such as the USA, Australia and New Zealand, the law on murder has been codified, usually with different 'degrees 'of murder to reflect the graduated levels of fault with which this offence can be committed. Because there is only one 'degree' of murder in England and Wales, there is only one sentence — the mandatory life sentence — and that means judges have limited scope to differentiate between types of murderers. The serial killer receives the same sentence as the gang member who kept a lookout and warned the actual killer of the victim's arrival.

The situation also results in 'mercy-killers' (who in truth are 'murderers') being convicted of the lesser offence of manslaughter by reason of diminished responsibility simply to avoid the mandatory sentence, and in 1989, the report of the Select Committee of the House of Lords on murder and life imprisonment agreed with most of the senior judges who had given evidence to the committee and recommended abolition of this sentence.

When imposing the life sentence, judges do have the power to set a 'tariff' — a minimum term that must be served before the defendant is eligible for parole — but although this allows some measure of differentiation between murderers, it is still the case that a life sentence is precisely that. Even though the great majority of 'lifers' are released early, they are only released on licence, which means they can be returned to prison if they commit any criminal offence later.

Intention

The greatest single criticism of the present law of murder is over the *mens rea*, which is described as malice aforethought, even though no malice (hatred or ill-will) or any premeditation are required. The *mens rea* for murder has been interpreted by judges to mean intention to kill or to commit GBH — see *R v Vickers* (1957) — but Professor Glanville Williams has asked: 'Why is it that intention, one of the basic concepts of the criminal law, remains so unclear? Judges decline to define it, and they appear to adjust it from one case to another.' This constant reinterpretation is most obvious in questions of oblique intent, where the definition has changed completely from the cases of *DPP v Smith* (1961), through *Hyam v DPP* (1975) and *R v Moloney* (1985), and then *R v Hancock and Shankland* (1986) to the current situation established in *R v Nedrick* (1986), *R v Woollin* (1999) and *R v Matthews and Alleyne* (2003). The present position is that the jury may find the intent necessary for a murder conviction if it is satisfied that the defendant foresaw death or serious injury as being a virtually certain consequence of his or her voluntary act or acts. In the case of *Woollin* (where the defendant's murder conviction was later quashed), the defendant was convicted of killing his baby son whom he had no desire whatever to kill.

A further critical issue is that of implied malice, where the defendant's intention was to commit GBH. In *R v Vickers*, Lord Goddard CJ defended this level of *mens rea* as always having been sufficient in English law to imply the malice aforethought for murder. However, it does have the unwelcome consequence of making murder in such cases an offence of constructive liability, where the *mens rea* does not correspond with the *actus reus* or with the punishment imposed for the offence. As Edmund-Davies LJ has noted, it cannot be right that a defendant who deliberately breaks the victim's arm, which then causes the victim's death, should be convicted of murder, and as the Criminal Law Revision Committee stated in its 1980 report: 'It is wrong in principle that a person should be liable to be convicted of murder who neither intended nor was reckless as to the most important element in the offence, namely death.'

Recommendations for future reform

The Law Commission has accepted these major criticisms and has recommended that there be two degrees of murder. The first degree would require intentional killing, or killing through an intention to do serious injury but with an awareness of a serious risk of causing death. Second-degree murder would involve killing with an intention to do serious injury, or killing where there was an awareness of the risk of causing death coupled with an intention to cause injury, a fear of injury or a risk of injury. If this particular recommendation is passed into law, at a stroke it will resolve the twin issues of the mandatory sentence and the 'intention' problem.

Voluntary manslaughter

The law on voluntary manslaughter has also given rise to considerable criticisms. First, the offence itself is an artificial one, created to enable murderers to escape the gallows on the grounds that their fault in killing was in some way reduced, either because of loss of self-control due to provocation or by diminished responsibility caused by an abnormality of mind. It is noteworthy that the Law Commission has recommended that, in future, defendants who successfully plead provocation or diminished responsibility will be convicted of second-degree murder rather than manslaughter; this acknowledges that the major justification for such defences is to avoid the mandatory life sentence.

Provocation

The plea of provocation is criticised as being biased towards men, who are more prone to lose their self-control than women, hence the controversial decisions in *R* v *Thornton* and *R* v *Ahluwalia* (both 1992). It is also criticised on the ground that part of the blame for the killing is placed on the victim. There has never been any attempt to restrict the type of conduct that constitutes provocation. In *R* v *Doughty* (1986), even a baby crying was held to be possible evidence of provocation. Judges have continually widened this defence to include cumulative provocation — *R* v *Humphreys* (1995) — and to extend the requirement of 'sudden and immediate loss of self-control', as in *R* v *Baillie* (1995).

The most serious criticism surrounds the 'reasonable man' test. By definition, of course, the reasonable person would never lose self-control to the extent that he or she would then kill. This test has been manipulated by judges in many different ways, as illustrated by the decisions in the cases of *R* v *Bedder* (1954), *DPP* v *Camplin* (1978), *R* v *Morhall* (1996), *R* v *Smith* (2000) and now *Attorney General for Jersey* v *Holley* (2005). Lord Nicholls in *Holley* referred to the 'mental gymnastics' required of juries in dealing with this test. If the defendant were a paedophile who had been taunted about this 'condition', the jury would have to be asked to consider the effect of these taunts on a 'reasonable man who was a paedophile' in terms of the gravity of the provocation. This is surely an impossible and wholly unrealistic task. The Law Commission proposes major changes in provocation to address the current problems, for example requiring the defendant to have acted in response to gross provocation that caused the defendant to have a justifiable sense of being seriously wronged or out of fear of serious violence.

Diminished responsibility

According to the Law Commission report 'Partial Defences to Murder', public opinion broadly supports 'treating in a tolerant way those who kill because of serious mental abnormality'. The principal argument in favour of retaining the partial defence of diminished responsibility, which the Law Commission recommends, is that of 'fair and just labelling' — the view being that it is 'unjust to label as murderers those not fully liable for their actions'. Professor Mackay stated: 'There is, in my view, a clear moral distinction between murder and a diminished responsibility killing despite the presence of the *mens rea* of the former offence.' Further arguments are that the full defence of insanity being seriously outdated reinforces the need for this partial defence, and that if this defence were not available, in some cases juries might acquit the defendant altogether.

However, there are certain key criticisms in relation to this partial defence to murder. The first of these is that the legal burden of proof rests on the defendant to prove the defence, albeit on the balance of probabilities. This breaches the 'golden rule' that it is for the prosecution to prove the defendant's guilt. For other defences, the defendant has only to produce evidence of those defences and it is then the duty of the prosecution to prove the absence of them. It has been argued that this placing of the burden of proof contravenes Article 6(2) of the **European Convention on Human Rights**, which guarantees the presumption of innocence and the imposition of the burden of proof on the prosecution.

A further serious criticism is directed at the categories that may produce a mental abnormality. According to Janet Loveless, writing in *Complete Criminal Law: Test, Cases, and Materials* (2008), these are:

> ...vague and problematic because psychiatrists have to testify to the presence of an abnormality of mind the formulation of which is not linked to a medical definition of mental illness. It is not a psychiatric term...the specified causes, as strictly interpreted, are rigid and would exclude the mercy-killer who kills through compassion under a temporary condition of mental imbalance, usually severe depression. This is because such depression is 'reactive' as opposed to 'organic'.

In many murder cases where diminished responsibility is pleaded, there will be a disagreement between psychiatrists called by the prosecution and those called by the defence — either as to whether or not there is an abnormality of mind, or as to whether the abnormality of mind 'substantially impaired the offender's mental responsibility'. How is a jury supposed to be able to determine which expert psychiatrist is correct? Especially, how can a jury assess whether the mental abnormality has substantially impaired the defendant's mental responsibility?

Critical evaluation of defences

Self-defence

At present, self-defence is an all-or-nothing defence. If it is successfully pleaded, the defendant will be acquitted; if not, the defendant will be convicted of the crime charged, and if that is murder, the mandatory life sentence must be imposed. In *R* v *Clegg* (1995), defence counsel argued before the House of Lords that in cases brought against police officers or, as in that particular case, military personnel assisting the civil powers, use of reasonable force should be capable of mitigating the offence so that what would otherwise be a murder conviction could be reduced to involuntary manslaughter. This had been recommended by the report of the Nathan Committee (House of Lords, 1989), but the argument was rejected by the Law Lords, on the grounds that such a change in the law could only be made by Parliament. In its report of 2006, 'Murder, Manslaughter and Infanticide', the Law Commission rejected making excessive-force self-defence a partial defence to murder, instead suggesting that a wider defence of provocation could address the problem by reducing first-degree murder to second-degree murder.

There has also been considerable public concern about the use of lethal force by the police in defence of state security. The mistaken shooting of Jean Charles de Menezes in London in 2005 clearly illustrates the reasons for this concern. Could such a killing be defended using the law on self-defence? And, if so, is such a law compatible with Article 2 — the right to life — in the **European Convention on Human Rights and Fundamental Freedoms** (ECHR)? Article 2 could also make it difficult to use self-defence to justify killing a person in defence of property, or in the more general prevention of crime. As Rebecca Huxley-Binns comments in *Criminal Law: the Fundamentals* (2007): 'It is difficult to imagine where a proportionate response to a threat to property is to kill.'

Insanity

The first criticism of the defence of insanity is that the rules were created by judges in 1843, when psychiatric illness was barely understood. Despite huge developments in understanding, diagnosing and treating psychiatric illness, the M'Naghten rules remain unchanged and an insanity plea must satisfy these rules as interpreted by judges. In 1953, the Royal Commission on Capital Punishment described these rules as obsolete and misleading, and the superficiality of 'disease of the mind' as outdated and inaccurate.

The present law can also be criticised for being too wide because it covers epilepsy, sleepwalking and diabetes; see *R* v *Sullivan* (1983), *R* v *Burgess* (1991) and *R* v *Hennessy* (1989). At the same time, it is too narrow as it can exclude many defendants who are clinically (but not legally) insane: the defect-of-reason test excludes those who know what they are doing but cannot help themselves.

Psychiatric medicine no longer defines mental disorders as insanity, and a psychiatrist would argue that a person may understand what he or she is doing and still be mentally ill, whereas a judge would hold that a person who is partially rational is not insane and therefore must be held accountable. As is the position with diminished responsibility, it is common for prosecution and defence to lead conflicting expert evidence at trial. If left to the jury by the trial judge, the decision of whether or not the defendant is legally insane is made by medically unqualified jurors, who have to choose between expert psychiatrists.

To detain under the **Criminal Procedure (Insanity and Unfitness to Plead) Act 1991** defendants who are epileptics, diabetics or sleepwalkers could be in breach of Article 5 of the ECHR — the right to liberty. In *Winterwerp v Netherlands* (1979), the European Court of Human Rights ruled that whether or not someone is of unsound mind is a matter of objective medical expertise and that detention is unlawful, unless the mental disorder warrants compulsory hospitalisation.

Finally, it can be argued that the M'Naghten rules are contrary to the presumption of innocence enshrined in Article 6 of the ECHR — the right to a fair trial — because the burden of proof is reversed. Since the prosecution is not required to prove *mens rea* in insanity cases, the criticism arises that, if the defendant fails to prove insanity but the prosecution proves the *actus reus*, the defendant can still be convicted, despite the existence of reasonable doubt concerning the *mens rea*.

Intoxication

In *Criminal Law: the Fundamentals*, Rebecca Huxley-Binns writes about the rules concerning intoxication as a defence: 'The law is a mass of inconsistency, lacks any logic and is rooted firmly in policy.'

In *Complete Criminal Law: Texts, Cases and Materials*, Janet Loveless argues that 'the Majewski rule is contrary to three fundamental principles of criminal liability:

> It assumes that recklessness in the ordinary sense of the word is a sufficient substitute for recklessness in the legal sense of the word. The latter requires awareness of the risk of committing the *actus reus* of an offence, whereas the former is a colloquial description of non-criminal conduct. Ashworth notes that, 'in most cases it is far-fetched to argue that a person who is getting drunk is aware of the type of conduct he or she might later indulge in' (*Principles of Criminal Law*).

> It ignores the principle that *actus reus* and *mens rea* should coincide. The recklessness in becoming drunk will usually occur before the crime is committed.

> It is contrary to the general principle that *mens rea* must be proved by the prosecution. It also runs counter to s.8 Criminal Justice Act 1967, which requires juries to consider the defendant's subjective state of mind. Clearly, if the defendant is so intoxicated as to not know what he is doing or fails to foresee something that they ordinarily would not miss, the defendant will have no 'state of mind' that could be described as one of *mens rea*.

A further criticism of the *Majewski* rule lies in the distinction it makes between crimes of basic and specific intent. It assumes that this distinction is always easy to draw, when this is simply not the case. Another problem arises with that part of the rule that allows the defendant to be convicted of a basic-intent offence if intoxication is accepted as a partial defence to a specific-intent crime. This functions in murder, where the defendant can be convicted of involuntary manslaughter, but in theft — a crime of specific intent — there is no lesser basic-intent offence.

Contract law

Formation of contract

In order to be valid, a contract must meet certain conditions, such as an offer and an acceptance, and these have to be present when it is formed. Bilateral contracts involve one party making an offer and another party indicating acceptance either orally or in writing. Unilateral contracts are where only one party is making a promise; an example is the case of *Carlill* v *Carbolic Smoke Ball Company* (1893), where one party made an offer but acceptance was through the performance of an act, rather than through a formal indication of acceptance.

Offer

An offer is defined as an expression of willingness to contract on certain terms, made with the intention that it will become binding on acceptance. An offer may be express or it may be implied from conduct, as when taking goods to the checkout in a supermarket.

An offer can be specific (made to one person or group of people, in which case it can only be accepted by that person or group) or it can be general and not limited as to whom it is directed at. An offer of a reward is a good example of a general offer, as in *Carlill* v *Carbolic Smoke Ball Company*; a more recent example is *Bowerman* v *ABTA* (1996), where the offer was that any holiday booked with a particular tour operator would be guaranteed by the Association of British Travel Agents if the tour operator ceased trading.

Examples of offers
- Reward posters and advertisements are offers, so long as it is clear that all that needs to be done is to fulfil certain conditions, as happened in *Carlill* v *Carbolic Smoke Ball Company*.
- Promotional campaigns, such as a supermarket's campaign to encourage customers to buy one product and get another free, are offers.

Possible offers
The law as to what constitutes an offer with regard to public transport and timetables remains unclear, but in *Wilkie* v *London Passenger Transport Board* (1947), it was suggested that the offer is made by running the service and the offer is accepted when the passenger gets on board.

Further rules about offers
- The offer must be certain, i.e. its terms must be clear and definite without any ambiguity.
- The offer can be made by any method. It can be made in writing, orally or by conduct (for example by picking up an item and taking it to the cash desk).
- The offer can be made to anyone — to an individual, a group, a company or organisation, and even, as in *Carlill* v *Carbolic Smoke Ball Company*, to the whole

world. As Lindley LJ commented in *Carlill*: 'The offer is to anybody who performs the conditions named in the advertisement.'

- The offer must be communicated because a person cannot accept what he or she does not know about.
- The offer must still be in existence when it is accepted. Any revocation must be received before the acceptance is made.

Termination of offers

An offer can be brought to an end at any point before acceptance in a number of different ways:

- **By acceptance or refusal:** acceptance may be in writing, orally or by conduct. If an offer is refused, it is ended, which means that it cannot be accepted later if there is a change of mind.
- **By failure of a precondition:** some offers are made subject to certain conditions, as when a person offers to sell his or her car if he or she is given a company car.
- **By a counter-offer:** as in *Hyde* v *Wrench* (1840).
- **By revocation:** withdrawal of the offer must be communicated, but that can be by a third party, as in *Dickinson* v *Dodds* (1876). The revocation must be received before the acceptance is made, as illustrated in *Byrne* v *Van Tienhoven* (1880). It seems that a revocation will be valid if it is delivered to the last known address. This would also appear to be the position if the revocation is sent by fax or telex during office hours but is not read until some time later. Where the offer is to enter into a unilateral contract, the revocation must take place before performance has begun; an exception to this rule is the promise to pay commission to estate agents for the sale of a property. To revoke an offer made to the public at large, it is probably sufficient to take reasonable steps to draw it to the attention of those at whom the original offer was directed.
- **By lapse of time:** where no time limit is specified, the offer will remain open for a reasonable time; see *Ramsgate Victoria Hotel* v *Montefiore* (1866). What is considered reasonable will depend on the circumstances, for example an offer to sell perishable goods may lapse in a few days. If a time limit is specified, it must be complied with.
- **By the death of the person making the offer:** it has been suggested that the death of either party terminates the offer, as it makes it impossible for the parties to reach agreement.

Acceptance

Acceptance is unqualified and unconditional agreement by words or conduct to all the terms of the offer. If conditions or qualifications are added, a counter-offer is created; see *Tinn* v *Hoffman* (1873).

Rules on acceptance

Acceptance must be communicated. Mere silence cannot amount to acceptance, unless it is absolutely clear that acceptance was intended; see *Felthouse* v *Bindley* (1862). Acceptance can be inferred from conduct. The principle seems to be that when you start to implement what is in the offer, you have accepted, but the courts will interpret conduct as indicating acceptance only if it seems reasonable to infer that acceptance was intended, as happened in *Brogden* v *Metropolitan Rail Co.* (1877).

Methods of acceptance

If a method of acceptance is specified, it must be complied with, but in some circumstances another, equally good, method may suffice. In *Tinn* v *Hoffman,* acceptance was requested by return of post, but the court held that 'any other means not later than a letter written by return of post' could be used. If no method is specified, any method will do, as long as it is effective. However, where an offer is made by an instantaneous method, such as e-mail, fax or telephone, an acceptance by post would not usually be considered reasonable.

The 'postal rule' applies when ordinary letter post is used. This means that acceptance is valid when posted, even if the letter is lost in the post, but a revocation of an offer is valid only when it is received; see *Adams* v *Lindsell* (1818), *Household Fire Insurance* v *Grant* (1879) and *Henthorn* v *Fraser* (1892). The postal rule does not apply where the person making the offer has specified that acceptance must be directly communicated, as in *Holwell Securities Ltd* v *Hughes* (1974).

Instantaneous methods

When instantaneous methods such as telephone, fax or telex are used, acceptance is immediate so long as the message is actually received; see *Entores* v *Miles Far East Corporation* (1955) and *Brinkibon* v *Stahag Stahl* (1983).

Standard-form contracts

If an offer is made by a business using its own standard form and the business receiving the offer alters the terms by sending back its own form, that second form amounts to a counter-offer. What may then follow is a series of communications, with each party referring to its own terms. The general rule in such cases is that the 'last shot' wins the battle; see *British Road Services* v *Arthur V. Crutchley and Co.* (1968) and contrast with *Butler Machine Tool Co.* v *Ex-Cell-O Corporation* (1979).

Consideration

Consideration is something of value being offered by each party. Sometimes it can be of little value, and it does not have to correspond to the actual worth of what the other party offers. Consideration was defined in *Currie* v *Misa* (1875) as 'some right, interest, profit or benefit accruing to one party, or some forbearance, detriment, loss or responsibility given, suffered or undertaken by the other'. It is possible to have a valid contract even if one party does not provide consideration, but only if the contract is made by deed.

Types of consideration

Consideration can, and often does, involve a promise by the parties to do something in the future, and this exchange of promises is called **executory consideration**. In unilateral contracts, however, the party making the offer, for example of a reward, is under no obligation until the other party performs (executes) his or her part of the agreement. This is called **executed consideration**.

Rules of consideration

- Something of value must be given by all the parties. This distinguishes a contract from a purely gratuitous agreement, i.e. a promise to make a gift. The law says that consideration must be sufficient. This means that it must be real and tangible and have some actual value.
- It does not have to be adequate, i.e. the market price. The courts will not investigate contracts to see if the parties have got equal value; see *Thomas* v *Thomas* (1842) and *Chappell and Co. Ltd* v *Nestlé Co. Ltd* (1959).
- It must not be past. Any consideration must come after the agreement, rather than being something that has already been done. For example, if A paints B's house and after the work is finished, B promises to pay £100 for it, this promise is unenforceable because A's consideration is past. An example is *Re McArdle* (1951). The law recognises, however, that there are situations in which something, for example a restaurant meal or a taxi ride, is provided on the unspoken expectation that ultimately it will be paid for. This principle is known as the rule in *Lampleigh* v *Braithwaite* (1615) and was applied in *Re Casey's Patent* (1892).
- It must not be an existing duty. Doing something that you are already bound to do cannot amount to good consideration; see *Stilk* v *Myrick* (1809) and contrast *Hartley* v *Ponsonby* (1857). The modern example of *Williams* v *Roffey* (1990) seems to indicate that, as regards business contracts, the courts will try to find consideration in circumstances where, on the face of it, the consideration appears to part of an existing duty. In other duty situations, such as *Glasbrook Brothers* v *Glamorgan County Council* (1925) and *Harris* v *Sheffield United Football Club* (1988), the courts have also been prepared to find evidence of consideration. A promise to do something as part of a contract, which the party is already obliged to do under a contract with a third party, can be good consideration: see *Scotson* v *Pegg* (1861).
- Part-payment of a debt cannot be consideration for the whole debt — see *Pinnel's Case* (1602) — unless something else is offered as consideration. There are, however, a number of exceptions to this rule.
- The **Contracts (Rights of Third Parties) Act 1999** has significantly altered the position of third parties who are beneficiaries of contracts. In the past, such contracts would not have been enforceable by the third parties as they had not supplied consideration; see *Tweddle* v *Atkinson*. Now s.1(1) of the 1999 Act allows a third party to enforce a contract if it contains an express term to that effect or if the contract purports to confer a benefit on a third party. The Act allows enforcement only where the benefit is intended for a specific person or for a member of a specific group and where it is clear that the parties intended the benefit to be enforceable by the third party.

Invitations to treat

An 'invitation to treat' is a preliminary stage at which someone is invited to make an offer. Whether something is an offer or an invitation will depend on all the circumstances.

The following are invitations to treat:

- displays of goods in shop windows, as in *Fisher* v *Bell* (1961)
- displays of goods in self-service stores, as in *Pharmaceutical Society* v *Boots* (1953)
- small advertisements, for example in magazines or newspapers, as in *Partridge* v *Crittenden* (1968)
- price lists, catalogues, circulars and timetables
- responses to requests for information, as in *Harvey* v *Facey* (1983), *Gibson* v *Manchester City Council* (1979)
- auction sales, as in *British Car Auctions* v *Wright* (1972)
- invitations to tender

Privity of contract

Privity of contract means that only a party to a contract can sue on it. This principle was set out by Viscount Haldane LC in *Dunlop Pneumatic Tyre Co.* v *Selfridge and Co.* (1915). There are a number of exceptions to the rule:
- Parliament is able to legislate to create third-party rights.
- Restrictive covenants bind subsequent purchasers, even though they were not parties to the original agreement; see *Tulk* v *Moxhay* (1848).
- Creation of a trust avoids the strict application of privity of contract, although the courts have been reluctant to accept that a trust exists when it is not explicitly stated.
- Where a collateral contract may be said to exist, as in *Shanklin Pier* v *Detel Products Ltd* (1951), privity of contract may be avoided.
- The court may identify a number of related contracts indicating a clear intention that benefits under the contract in question were to be shared between members of a family or of some other group; see *Jackson* v *Horizon Holidays* (1975), although this was not approved by the House of Lords in *Woodar Investment Development Ltd* v *Wimpey Construction Ltd* (1980).
- The **Contracts (Rights of Third Parties) Act 1999** allows a third party to enforce a contract (see the rules of consideration on p. 45).

Intention to create legal relations

Social and domestic agreements
Case law suggests that agreements within families will not generally be treated as legally binding; see *Jones* v *Padavatton* (1969). Contrast *Balfour* v *Balfour* (1919) and *Merritt* v *Merritt* (1970). In cases that do not simply involve members of the same family, any presumption that the arrangement is a purely social one will be rebutted if money has changed hands; see *Simpkins* v *Pays* (1955), *Peck* v *Lateu* (1973) and *Parker* v *Clarke* (1960).

Commercial and business agreements
There is a strong presumption that in commercial agreements, the parties intend to be legally bound, as was confirmed in *Esso Petroleum* v *Customs and Excise Commissioners* (1976). There are, however, a number of circumstances in which a different intent can be shown: honour clauses are one such exception (see *Roes and Frane* v *Crompton Bros*,

1925), and football pools (as in *Jones* v *Vernon Pools*, 1938), are another. Situations where free gifts or prizes are promised are deemed to be legally binding because the purpose is to promote the commercial interests of the body offering the gift or prize; see *McGowan* v *Radio Buxton* (2001). In *Edwards* v *Skyways* (1964), an ex-gratia payment, i.e. a gift, by an airline was held to be related to business matters and was presumed to be binding.

Contract terms

Statements that are incorporated into the contract and by which the parties intend to be bound are known as **terms**. A statement intended to induce or persuade a party to enter into a contract is not a term, but a **representation**, and so long as it is not incorporated into the contract, it remains a representation. It should be noted, however, that, because of the **Misrepresentation Act 1967**, this distinction is of less practical significance than it was.

In order to become a term, a statement must be incorporated and form part of the contract. Whether or not it is incorporated depends on a number of factors:
- If a party attaches importance to a statement and has relied on it when deciding to enter into the contract, it will probably be treated as forming part of the contract, as in *Birch* v *Paramount Estates Ltd* (1956).
- The courts are more likely to treat a statement by an expert as incorporated into the contract than a statement by someone without specialist knowledge. Contrast *Oscar Chess Ltd* v *Williams* (1957) and *Dick Bentley Productions Ltd* v *Harold Smith Motors Ltd* (1965).
- The nearer in time the statement is to the formation of the contract, the more likely the court is to treat it as having been incorporated; see *Routledge* v *McKay* (1954).
- A statement is more likely to be deemed a term if it is in writing.
- The more the statement has been drawn to the other party's attention, the more likely it is to be regarded as a term.
- Under the 'parol evidence' rule, oral or other evidence that a party tries to introduce into a written agreement is not admissible to add to, vary or contradict the terms in the written contract; see *Henderson* v *Arthur* (1907). However, there are occasions when strict enforcement of this rule is not appropriate, for example where it is unfair because one party is trying to take advantage of the other's mistake, as in *Webster* v *Cecil* (1861). A collateral contract is another way in which an oral statement can be deemed to be a term, and therefore binding, even though it conflicts with a written statement.

Conditions and warranties

Conditions are terms that are fundamental to the contract, that go to its root. A breach of a condition will give the injured party the choice of either repudiating (ending) the contract or continuing with it and claiming damages.

Warranties are less important terms and, if broken, entitle an injured party only to damages.

Is a term a condition or warranty?
- The distinction between conditions and warranties can be illustrated by two cases involving opera singers. In *Bettini* v *Gye* (1876), the breach was minor and was therefore treated as a warranty, while in *Poussard* v *Spiers and Pond* (1876), the breach was an important one and was treated as a condition.
- Written contracts may specify that particular terms are conditions, and this is likely to reflect the intention of the parties to treat certain terms as more important than others, as in *Lombard North Central* v *Butterworth* (1987). The courts, however, are not bound to treat the terms in the way a contract describes them. An example is *L Schuler AG* v *Wickman Machine Tool Sales* (1973).
- The implied terms in sections 12–15 of the **Sale of Goods Act 1979** (as amended) are described in the statute as conditions or warranties. These statutory provisions are not negotiable and it is not open to the parties or the courts to alter their status.
- If the parties themselves do not label terms as conditions or warranties, the courts decide the matter on a case-by-case basis.

Innominate terms
Following the decision of the Court of Appeal in *Hong Kong Fir Shipping Co* v *Kawasaki Kisen Kaisha Ltd* (1962), contracts may also include innominate terms. These are terms that are regarded as more important than warranties but less important than conditions; when broken, they give rise to a claim for damages and, when seriously breached to the detriment of one of the parties, they entitle him or her to repudiate the contract.

Express terms

Wherever possible, when the courts have to determine the meaning of a contractual term, words are given their natural and ordinary meaning, but sometimes the courts will look beyond this when a strict interpretation goes against what seems to be a sensible interpretation. In a number of recent decisions, the Law Lords, and Lord Hoffmann in particular, have developed an approach characterised by flexibility and a desire to find the meaning that would make sense to a reasonable person; see, for example *Sirius International Insurance Co.* v *FAI General Insurance Ltd* (2004).

Implied terms

Terms that are implied are those that, it is assumed, both parties would have intended to include if they had thought about it. They may have thought that a particular term was so obvious that it was not necessary to refer to it or they may have left it out by mistake.

The law has developed two tests to determine whether a term should be written into a contract. The first is known as the 'officious bystander' test — whether the term is one that a third party, standing by, would have thought was obviously intended by the contracting parties. The test originates from remarks by MacKinnon LJ in *Shirlaw* v

Southern Foundries (1939). He said that a term may be implied 'if it is so obvious that it goes without saying'. One situation in which the 'officious bystander' test cannot be used is where one of the parties would not have understood the term if it had been there, as in *Spring* v *National Amalgamated Stevedores and Dockers Society* (1956). Another situation where the test will not apply is where it is clear that one of the parties would not have agreed to the term if it had been discussed; see *Luxor (Eastbourne) Ltd* v *Cooper* (1941).

The other test is the business efficiency test, where the question is whether a term must be implied in order for the contract to work as an effective business arrangement. The leading case is *The Moorcock* (1889).

Terms implied by custom or trade usage
Terms can be implied if there is evidence that, under local custom, they would normally be there, or if they would routinely be part of a contract in a particular type of trade or business, as in *British Crane Hire Corporation Ltd* v *Ipswich Plant Hire Ltd* (1975).

Implied terms created by statute
Implied terms have also been created by statute. Section 2(1) of the **Sale of Goods Act 1979**, for example, which applies to a sale of goods, defines a contract of sale of goods as 'a contract by which the seller transfers or agrees to transfer the property in goods to the buyer for a money consideration, called the price'. The term 'goods' has been interpreted to include packaging and any instructions appearing on the packaging. Certain provisions of the Act apply only when goods are sold 'in the course of a business'. In *Stevenson* v *Rogers* (1999), a fisherman, whose normal business was selling fish, sold his boat. The Court of Appeal held that this was still a sale in the course of a business.

Section 12(1) of the 1979 Act says that, in a contract of sale, there is an implied term that the seller has the right to sell the goods and is able to pass good title; see *Rowland* v *Divall* (1923). Section 13(1) provides that, where there is a sale of goods by description, there is an implied term that the goods will correspond with the description, as illustrated in *Beale* v *Taylor* (1967) and *Varley* v *Whipp* (1900). However, there must be reliance on the description; see *Harlington and Leinster Enterprises* v *Christopher Hull Fine Art* (1991). Enforcement of s.13 is strict, as illustrated by *Re Moore and Landauer* (1921), but *Reardon Smith Line* v *Hansen-Tangen* (1976) suggests that a trivial breach of description would not be sufficient to allow a party to repudiate the contract. Note that this implied term is not limited to sales in the course of business and therefore also applies to private sales.

Section 14(2) of the 1979 Act, as amended by s.1 of the **Sale and Supply of Goods Act 1994**, says that where a seller sells goods in the course of a business, there is an implied term that the goods are of satisfactory quality. Note that this does not apply to private sales. Under s.14(2)(a), 'goods are of satisfactory quality if they meet the standard that a reasonable person would regard as satisfactory, taking account of any description of the goods, the price (if relevant) and all the other relevant circumstances'. Potentially relevant factors outlined under s.14(2)(b) are: fitness for the purpose for which goods of this kind are commonly supplied, finish and appearance, freedom from minor defects, safety and durability. Cases illustrating 'satisfactory quality' are *Priest* v *Last* (1903) and *Bartlett* v *Sidney Marcus* (1965).

In *Brown* v *Craiks* (1970), Lord Reid commented that if you pay a higher price, then you can expect higher quality. This was confirmed in *Clegg* v *Andersson* (2003). The goods need to be satisfactory in their entirety; see *Wilson* v *Rickett, Cockerell and Co.* (1954). A buyer cannot later claim that goods are unsatisfactory if the defect is specifically brought to his or her attention before the contract is made or if he or she examines the goods (or a sample of them if it is a contract for sale by sample) before contracting, and the defect is one that he or she should have discovered on examining them (s.14(2)(c)). This is illustrated by *Bramhill* v *Edwards* (2004).

Section 14(3) states that there is an implied term that goods are fit for any purpose that the buyer specifically makes known to the seller, unless the buyer does not rely on the seller's judgement or it would be unreasonable for him or her to do so; see *Griffiths* v *Peter Conway* (1939). This section applies only to sales in the course of a business and not to private sales.

Section 15 says that there are implied terms that where goods are sold by sample, the bulk must correspond to sample, and that the goods will be free from any defect making their quality unsatisfactory that would not be apparent on reasonable examination of the sample.

Exclusion of implied terms

Under the **Unfair Contract Terms Act 1977**, s.12 of the **Sale of Goods Act 1979** (as amended) cannot be excluded from any contract, while sections 13–15 cannot be excluded from consumer contracts, and can only be excluded from other contracts if this is reasonable.

Remedies for breach of implied terms

Right to repudiate

A breach of an implied term is a breach of condition, and allows the purchaser to reject the goods and demand the return of the purchase price. This right to reject is lost once the goods have been accepted, and the claim then is limited to damages; see s.11(4) of the 1979 Act. Section 61 provides that the remedy in such cases is damages.

Under s.35, acceptance occurs when the buyer intimates acceptance to the seller, when the buyer does something inconsistent with the seller's ownership after he or she has had a chance to examine the goods (as in the 1893 case of *Perkins* v *Bell*), or when the buyer retains the goods after the lapse of a reasonable time without indicating to the seller that he or she is rejecting them. Sections 2(5) and 2(6) of the **Sale and Supply of Goods Act 1994** state that the buyer must have reasonable opportunity to examine goods and that even having goods repaired by or under arrangement with the seller may not amount to acceptance. Contrasting cases on the treatment of acceptance are *Bernstein* v *Pamson Motors* (1987) and *Rogers* v *Parish (Scarborough) Ltd* (1987).

Under s.3 of the **Sale and Supply of Goods Act 1994**, there is a right of partial rejection where a defect affects only some of the goods and the buyer accepts the remainder.

Section 15(a) of the Act also added the provision that in consumer sales, the right to reject is lost when the breach is so slight that rejection would be unreasonable.

Right to damages

Damages may be more appropriate than rejection when supplies of a product are limited and buying an alternative is difficult, or where consumers have suffered personal injury because of a faulty product and wish to sue for consequential loss. The consumer will often be awarded sums far exceeding the value of the product itself, as in *Grant* v *Australian Knitting Mills* (1936) and *Godley* v *Perry* (1960). Another circumstance where damages may be appropriate is where the consumer has lost the right to reject by virtue of accepting the product.

Additional remedies

Under the **Sale and Supply of Goods to Consumers Regulations 2002**, consumers can request either repair of goods or replacement. The retailer can decline either of these requests if he or she can show that they would be disproportionately costly in comparison with the alternative. Any remedy must be completed without significant inconvenience to the consumer, and if neither repair nor replacement is realistically possible, consumers can request instead a partial or full refund, depending on what is reasonable in the circumstances.

The **Supply of Goods and Services Act 1982** extends the protection of implied terms under the **Sale of Goods Act 1979** to goods supplied as part of a service and also to goods that are hired. In addition, it sets out implied terms in relation to contracts for services. Where goods are supplied as part of a service, the implied terms specified in the Sale of Goods Act apply to the goods. For example, the paint and wallpaper used by a decorator or the fittings installed by a plumber are now covered by the Sale of Goods Act implied terms, which are restated in the 1982 Act (with title covered by s.2, description by s.3, satisfactory quality and fitness for purpose by s.4 and sample by s.5). In sections 7–10, the same implied terms are extended to any contract for hire of goods, for example the hire of a car or a television. There are some situations where it is not clear whether a contract is for the sale of goods or for services. Contrast *Lockett* v *A and M Charles Ltd* (1938) and *Robinson* v *Graves* (1935).

Under sections 13–15 of the **Supply of Goods and Services Act 1982**, certain specific terms are automatically implied in service contracts. These are referred to in the Act simply as terms rather than as conditions. They are therefore treated by the courts as innominate terms, and the consequences of a breach depend on how serious that breach is. Section 13 provides: 'In a contract for the supply of a service where the supplier is acting in the course of a business, there is an implied term the supplier will carry out the service with reasonable care and skill.' The reasonableness standard is similar to that used in cases of negligence and essentially requires the consumer to show not that a service was defective, but rather that the provider was at fault in the way it was provided; see *Wilson* v *Best Travel* (1993).

Section 14 creates the duty to carry out the service within a reasonable time. What is a reasonable time is a question of fact; see *Charnock* v *Liverpool Corporation* (1968).

Section 15 implies a term that, where the price has not been provided for by the contract or by a course of dealing, the customer will pay the supplier a reasonable charge. What is a reasonable charge is a question of fact.

Exemption clauses

Exemption clauses are terms in a contract that seek to exclude all liability in certain events or to limit the liability of one of the parties to a specific amount of money smaller than any reasonable pre-estimate of loss. They can be part of a prewritten document or a separate notice, or even agreed by the parties orally. Suppliers of goods and services often seek to exclude or limit their possible legal liability by the insertion of these clauses in their standard form contracts.

Common law controls

Where an exemption clause is contained in a document that has been signed, it automatically forms part of the contract. The signer is presumed to have read and understood the significance of all the terms contained in the document. This is known as the rule in *L'Estrange* v *Graucob* (1934). Note that this rule will not be held to apply if the other party has misrepresented the terms of the agreement, as happened in *Curtis* v *Chemical Cleaning and Dyeing Co.* (1951). For a signature to be effective in incorporating terms, the document signed must be regarded as contractual. A mere receipt or piece of paper for some other purpose is not enough. The exemption clause may also be contained in an unsigned document such as a ticket or notice, but in those cases the burden of showing that the terms have been incorporated is on the party seeking to rely on them.

For exemption clauses to be effective, the document containing them must be capable of being regarded by a reasonable person as contractual in nature and, as such, likely to contain exemption clauses; see *Chapelton* v *Barry UDC* (1940) and contrast *Parker* v *SE Railway* (1877). The person seeking to rely on the exemption clause must show that reasonable steps have been taken to give notice of the clause to the other contracting party. Denning LJ commented in *Spurling* v *Bradshaw* (1956):

> ...the more unreasonable a clause is, the greater the notice which must be given of it. Some clauses would need to be printed in red ink with a red hand pointing to it before the notice could be held to be sufficient.

Exemption clauses will also be ineffective unless notice of them is given before the contract is made or at the time the contact is made; see *Chapelton* v *Barry UDC*, *Olley* v *Marlborough Court Ltd* (1949) and *Thornton* v *Shoe Lane Car Parking Ltd* (1971). In *Hollier* v *Rambler Motors Ltd* (1972), a garage tried to rely on an exclusion clause in a notice displayed inside the garage, but the court decided that the customer did not go to the garage frequently enough to have established a course of dealings within which he would have had the opportunity to read the terms.

Where an exemption clause is duly incorporated into a contract, the courts will proceed to examine the words used to see if the clause covers the breach and loss that have occurred. An exemption clause will be effective only if it expressly covers the kind of liability that has, in fact, arisen. If there is any ambiguity or doubt as to the meaning of an exemption clause, the court will interpret it *contra proferentem*, i.e. against the interests of the person seeking to rely on it; see *Houghton* v *Trafalgar Insurance Co.* (1954).

Unfair Contract Terms Act 1977

The **Unfair Contract Terms Act 1977** is the most important piece of legislation affecting exemption clauses: it applies to contract terms and to notices that are non-contractual and purport to exclude or restrict liability in tort. Most of the Act's provisions apply only to things done in the course of business or arising from the occupation of premises used for business purposes (the term 'business' including the professions, government and local and public authorities). Many of the provisions apply only where one of the parties is contracting as a consumer. Under s.12(1), a person 'deals as a consumer' if:

(a) he or she does not make the contract in the course of a business or represent that he or she is doing so

(b) the other party does make the contract in the course of a business

(c) the goods are of a type ordinarily supplied for private use or consumption

In *Peter Symmons and Co.* v *Cook* (1981), the sale of a Rolls-Royce to a firm of surveyors was held to be a consumer sale.

Exemption clauses void under the 1977 Act

- In a consumer sale, s.6 of the 1977 Act, as amended, makes void any clause that tries to exclude or limit the implied terms in the **Sale of Goods Act 1979**.
- In any contract, s.6 of the 1977 Act, as amended, makes void any clause that tries to exclude or limit the implied term relating to title under s.12 of the **Sale of Goods Act 1979**.
- In a consumer sale, s.6 of the 1977 Act makes void exemption clauses relating to implied terms as to description (under s.13 of the **Sale of Goods Act 1979**), satisfactory quality (s.14(2) of the 1979 Act), fitness for purpose (s.14(3)) and sample corresponding with bulk (s.15). Section 6(4) extends the application of s.6 to hire purchase agreements.
- Section 2 of the 1977 Act makes void clauses in any contract, or any non-contractual notice, seeking to exempt liability for death or injury caused by negligence. This particularly applies to situations involving the provision of a service where there is an attempt to exclude s.13 of the **Supply of Goods and Services Act 1982**, which requires work to be done with reasonable care and skill.
- Section 5 of the 1977 Act makes void a manufacturer's guarantee seeking to exempt liability for loss or damage caused by defects in the goods while they are in consumer use.

Exemption clauses that seek to exclude or limit liability for negligent loss or damage in consumer contracts or between businesses will be valid only if reasonable (s.2 of the 1977 Act). Exemption clauses in contracts between businesses that seek to exclude or limit implied terms will also be valid only if reasonable (s.6(3)). This also applies to certain other clauses in consumer contracts or contracts between businesses where written standard terms are used (s.3) and to clauses that seek to exclude or restrict liability for misrepresentation (s.8).

What is reasonable?

The test of reasonableness is found in s.11 and Schedule 2 of the 1977 Act. The burden of proof is on the party inserting the clause to show that it is reasonable in all the circumstances, as illustrated in *Warren* v *Truprint Ltd* (1986). Under s.11(1), the court should ask whether the term is fair and reasonable, 'having regard to the circumstances which were, or ought reasonably to have been, known to or in the contemplation of the parties when the contract was made'. Schedule 2 of the Act refers to some potentially relevant issues, including the relative strength of the parties' bargaining positions and whether the customer received an inducement to agree to the term (for example a cheaper price). *Smith* v *Eric Bush* (1990), *Green* v *Cade* (1978) and *George Mitchell* v *Finney Lock Seeds* (1983) are cases where clauses were held to be unreasonable. In *Watford Electronics* v *Sanderson* (2001), the clause was found to be reasonable.

Generally, exemption clauses in consumer contracts are less likely than those in business contracts to satisfy the test of reasonableness, but if they are well drafted and placed in the right context, they may be held to be reasonable, as in *Woodman* v *Photo Trade Processing* (1981).

The Unfair Terms in Consumer Contracts Regulations 1999

These 1999 rules apply to any terms in contracts with consumers. They therefore cover not only unfair exemption clauses, but also any other type of clause considered to be unfair. A consumer is defined in Regulation 3(1) as 'any natural person...acting for purposes which are outside his trade, business or profession'. The regulations apply to terms that have not been individually negotiated (Regulation 5(1)), but they do not apply (Regulation 6(2)) to terms defining the main subject matter of the contract, or to the adequacy of the price or remuneration for goods or services provided.

Regulation 5(1) states that a term will be regarded as unfair if, 'contrary to the requirement of good faith, it causes a significant imbalance...to the detriment of the consumer'. The unfairness of a term is to be assessed under Regulation 6(1) by taking into account the nature of the goods or services, the circumstances under which the contract was made and any other contractual terms on which it is dependent. For a term to be unfair, the significant imbalance it creates must be contrary to good faith. Parties are required to deal with each other in an open and honest way, taking into account their relative bargaining strengths.

Misrepresentation

Misrepresentation is a **vitiating factor**. This means it has the effect of invalidating consent. A contract may be declared void on grounds of misrepresentation (which may be fraudulent, negligent or innocent). A misrepresentation is an untrue statement of fact that induces a party to enter a contract but is not itself part of the contract.

Statement of fact

To avoid a contract, misrepresentation does not have to be verbal. Conduct may be sufficient, for example payment by cheque if the payer knows that his or her bank will not honour the cheque. Lord Campbell LC in *Walters* v *Morgan* (1861), referred to 'a nod, a wink, a shake of the head or a smile' qualifying as statements. The general rule is that silence as to relevant facts does not amount to misrepresentation — there is no liability for failing to disclose them to the other party. In *Peek* v *Gurney* (1873), Lord Cairns stated: 'Mere non-disclosure of material facts, however morally censurable, would form no ground for an action for misrepresentation.' However, if a party makes any representation on a particular matter, it must be full and frank — silence may not be used to distort a positive representation. A half-true statement, which is accurate as far as it goes but conveys a misleading impression by being incomplete, may give rise to a misrepresentation, as in *Dimmock* v *Hallett* (1866) and *Spice Girls Ltd* v *Aprilia* (2000). With contracts that demand *uberrima fides* (utmost good faith) — for example insurance contracts — parties are bound to disclose all material facts, whether or not they are asked about them.

A misrepresentation must be distinguished from a mere commendation, a statement of opinion (see the 1927 case of *Bisset* v *Wilkinson*) and a statement of future intention, but note that a statement of future intention can become a misrepresentation if, as in *Edgington* v *Fitzmaurice* (1885), it is proved that there was no intention to do the promised act at the time the statement was made.

Inducing a party to enter a contract

For misrepresentation to be proved, it must be shown that the relevant statement induced the party who is now complaining to enter the contract. This is particularly important where the party to whom the statement was made was in a position to check its truth for himself or herself; see *Attwood* v *Small* (1838). The misrepresentation does not have to be the only reason why the other party entered the contract, but there must be reliance on the statement.

Types of misrepresentation

Fraudulent misrepresentation

Fraudulent misrepresentation occurs when a party makes a false statement without honestly believing it to be true. It may be a deliberate lie, or it may be a statement made recklessly. The classic definition outlined by the House of Lords in *Derry* v *Peek* (1889) is a false statement made 'without belief in its truth, or recklessly as to whether it is true or false'.

Negligent misrepresentation

Following the rule in *Hedley Byrne* v *Heller* (1964), success when claiming negligent misrepresentation depends upon proof of a special relationship existing between the parties. The principle of liability is based on the duty of care in tort. Section 2(1) of the **Misrepresentation Act 1967** provides that a non-fraudulent misrepresentation will be treated in the same way as a fraudulent one, unless the person making it 'proves that he had reasonable ground to believe and did believe up to the time the contract was made the facts represented were true'. The burden placed on the defendant by the 1967 Act to prove that it was reasonable to believe and that he or she did believe in the truth of the statements may be difficult to discharge, as was shown in *Howard Marine and Dredging Co.* v *Ogden and Sons* (1978).

Innocent misrepresentation

For a misrepresentation to have been made innocently, the person making it has to have an honest belief in its truth, for example where repeating inaccurate information supplied by someone else. Even in this case, it may be possible to bring an action in equity for rescission.

Remedies for misrepresentation

Rescission

This is an equitable remedy, which sets the contract aside and puts the parties back in the position they were in before the contract was made. It is available for all types of misrepresentation.

The injured party can rescind the contract by notifying the other party, or if this is not possible because of the behaviour of the other party, the injured party will need to take some reasonable action to indicate the intention to rescind; see *Car and Universal Finance* v *Caldwell* (1965).

Rescission will not be ordered where it is impossible to return the parties to their original pre-contract positions. This would most obviously happen where the subject matter of the contract has been used up or destroyed, as was the case in *Vigers* v *Pike* (1842). Rescission cannot be ordered where a third party has acquired rights under the contract, as in *White* v *Garden* (1851).

Damages

Damages are available in circumstances where rescission is not an adequate remedy, as when some kind of consequential loss has occurred, for example the failure of a cooling system with the resulting loss of foodstuffs in storage. Damages for misrepresentation are calculated on the same basis as they are in tort, with the aim of putting the parties back in the position they were in before the misrepresentation was made.

Exclusion of liability for misrepresentation

Section 3 of the **Misrepresentation Act 1967**, as amended by s.8 of the **Unfair Contract Terms Act 1977**, provides that terms that seek to exclude liability for a misrepresentation are valid only if reasonable.

Discharge of contract

A contract can be discharged, i.e. come to an end, in a number of ways:

- performance
- agreement
- frustration
- breach

Performance

The law expects performance of the terms of a contract to be exact and complete, and both parties must carry out their obligations under the contract; see *Re Moore and Landauer* (1921) and *Cutter* v *Powell* (1795). However, the courts do recognise the idea of substantial performance, which is where the work is almost completed and any minor defects can easily be corrected. In practice, therefore, it is a question of degree; contrast *Hoenig* v *Isaacs* (1952) and *Bolton* v *Mahadeva* (1972). Partial performance is where some work has been done, but it is insufficient to amount to substantial performance. In *Sumpter* v *Hedges* (1898), a builder left houses and stables only half-constructed and the claimant had no choice but to have the work finished; this was, therefore, not partial performance. Completion by a third party is known as vicarious performance. The rule is that vicarious performance is acceptable in situations that are not of a personal nature, provided that all the other terms of the contract are met. Where personal, individual skills are involved, for example the painting of a portrait, vicarious performance is unlikely to be appropriate; see *Edwards* v *Newland* (1950).

Agreement

This occurs where a contract is abandoned or its terms are varied by agreement. Both parties enter into a new agreement and both must, therefore, provide consideration if the agreement is to be valid.

Frustration

This arises when an event occurs, during the lifetime of the contract, which is not the fault of either party and which makes completion of the contract:

- impossible, for example in *Morgan* v *Manser* (1948), and in *Taylor* v *Caldwell* (1863), where a music hall was hired for a series of concerts, but before the concert dates arrived, the hall was destroyed by fire
- illegal (perhaps due to a new statute or the outbreak of war)
- radically different (as when the postponement of the coronation of Edward VII meant that some contracts no longer had any point — contrast the 1903 cases of *Herne Bay Steamboat Co.* v *Hutton* and *Krell* v *Henry*).

Note that the substance of the agreement must be undermined — it is not sufficient that completion is made more difficult or expensive, and the courts have to determine whether the frustration is genuine; see *Davis Contractors* v *Fareham UDC* (1956). A contract that is frustrated comes to an end automatically as soon as the frustrating event occurs, and without further action by either party. All further obligations are then annulled, but the contract is not in itself void and past obligations generally remain in force. Section 1(2) of the **Law Reform (Frustrated Contracts) Act 1943** gives a right to recover money already paid under such a contract and to withhold anything still payable, and s.1(3) provides that, where a party has received some valuable benefit (other than the payment of money) under the contract before its discharge, the court may order him or her to make an appropriate payment to the other party.

Breach

An actual breach is where there is a failure to fulfil an obligation under the contract or to fulfil it to the required standard; see the case of *Pilbrow* v *Pearless de Rougemont and Co.* (1999). Anticipatory breach occurs at some time before performance is due, when one party shows by express words or by implications from his or her conduct that he or she does not intend to observe his or her obligations under the contract; this principle was established in *Hochster* v *De La Tour* (1853). The party injured by an anticipatory breach of contract has the option of waiting for the performance date to pass and then suing for breach; see *Avery* v *Bowden* (1855).

The effects of breach of contract

The rights of the injured party depend on the nature of the term broken. A breach of a condition is a breach of an important term, giving the right to terminate the agreement and repudiate (cancel) the contract. A breach of a warranty is a breach of a minor term, which does not go to the root of the contract, and gives rise only to a claim for damages. Where the breach is of an innominate term in a contract, if the results are so serious as to undermine the very foundation of the contract, the innocent party has the right to terminate the contract. The contract is not automatically ended by the breach, as the innocent party can choose whether to treat the contract as discharged or opt to continue with it.

An injured party may not always be able to insist on affirming the contract because, under the principle of mitigation of loss, the injured party usually has a general duty to take reasonable steps to minimise his loss. There are three rules on mitigation:

(1) A claimant cannot recover for loss that could have been avoided by taking reasonable steps.

(2) A claimant cannot recover for any loss that has actually been avoided, even if he or she went further than was necessary in compliance with the above rule.

(3) A claimant may recover extra loss incurred in taking reasonable but unsuccessful steps to mitigate loss.

In *British Westinghouse* v *Underground Electric Railways Co. of London* (1912), it was said that a claimant mitigating loss would not be expected to 'take any step which a reasonable and prudent man would not ordinarily take in the course of his business'.

Remedies for breach of contract
Damages

The purpose of damages, as stated in *Robinson* v *Harman* (1848), is that 'when a party sustains loss by reason of a breach of contract he is, so far as money can do it, to be placed in the same situation with respect to damages as if the contract had been performed'. For damages to be awarded, there must be a causal link between the breach of contract and the damage suffered, and this is a question of fact in each case. The courts have to decide how far the losses suffered by the injured party should be recoverable. The principle used is that losses are recoverable if they are reasonably within the contemplation of the parties as a probable result of the breach. This principle is known as the rule in *Hadley* v *Baxendale* (1854). The application of the principle is illustrated by the case of *Victoria Laundry* v *Newman Industries* (1949).

Sometimes the parties agree in advance what would be reasonable compensation in the event of a breach, and this is referred to as **liquidated damages**. The courts will accept this sum only if it represents an accurate and proper assessment of loss. If not, it will be treated as a 'penalty' and be unenforceable; see *Dunlop Pneumatic Tyre Co.* v *New Garage and Motor Co.* (1915).

Damages that have not been agreed to in advance are known as **unliquidated damages**, and they will be determined by the court. Courts can award:
* **substantial damages** (a sum designed to compensate for actual losses suffered, which is the usual basis on which damages are calculated)
* **nominal damages** (a small sum, indicating that, although technically the party has a claim, the court does not feel that actual compensation is appropriate; see the 1830 case of *Staniforth* v *Lyall*)
* **exemplary damages** (a much larger sum than would be needed to compensate the injured party, to demonstrate the court's disapproval of the party at fault)

Because the aim of damages is to put the injured party as far as possible in the position he or she would have been in if the contract had been performed properly, damages are assessed depending on the circumstances of the case. The sum awarded may be based on the difference in value between the goods or services contracted for and the value of those actually delivered, or on the difference between the contract price and the market price if goods have to be obtained or sold elsewhere. In certain circumstances, damages may be awarded for intangible loss such as mental distress. In *Cook* v *Spanish Holiday Tours* (1960), damages for loss of enjoyment were paid to a honeymoon couple who were left without a room on their wedding night.

Equitable remedies

Unlike damages, the equitable remedies of injunction and specific performance are discretionary and are awarded by the court only if the circumstances of the case warrant it. Their use is appropriate when the award of damages would be inadequate and unjust. An injunction may also be an appropriate remedy to prevent someone from acting in breach of contract, for example by enforcing a contract in restraint of trade or a provision protecting trade secrets or specialist information.

'Specific performance' is an order of the court to make a party carry out his or her obligations under a contract, but it is appropriate only in situations where the subject matter of the contract is unique in some way, as in *Falcke* v *Gray* (1859), where the contract concerned a valuable work of art.

Critical evaluation of contract law

In this examination paper, Question 3 requires candidates to evaluate how effectively the law operates. This question needs to be approached in a different way from the other two parts. It is important to plan in advance the kind of comments that you intend to make and then adapt them to suit the actual question that is asked. It is likely that there will be an evaluation question on some aspect of formation of contract. Evaluation of offer and acceptance is generally the most popular question with candidates because there is such a lot to discuss, but it would also be prudent to prepare an answer on consideration or intention to create legal relations.

Offer and acceptance

In some situations, it is difficult to determine what constitutes an offer. The case of *Clarke* v *Dunraven* (1897), for example, does not seem to fit with the conventional idea of offer and acceptance. In that case, entering a yacht race created a contract between all the competitors. The House of Lords agreed that there was a contract, yet there was no specific offer and acceptance between individual competitors.

Are the rules that distinguish offers from invitations satisfactory? A good answer will briefly outline the relevant rules and comment on them. Are the cases decided appropriately? Probably most people will agree that the rules on self-service stores are sensible, but what about the outcome of *Fisher* v *Bell*? There is still some confusion in deciding whether some things, such as timetables and tickets for transport, are offers or invitations to treat. Another issue is the difficulty in distinguishing between counter-offers and requests for information. Refer back to the rules and decide whether you think they are sufficiently clear.

Because in unilateral contracts acceptance can be through conduct, it may not always be clear when performance that amounts to acceptance has started. Arguably, it would be unfair in many situations to allow acceptance to be valid from the first act. For example, looking for a lost item but not finding it would not be performance, but perhaps, once it is found, even if not yet returned, performance has begun. Equally, it would be unfair for an offeror to revoke his or her offer when the offeree has already done a substantial amount of work in response to it. The Law Commission in 1975 declared that an offer which the offeror has said will be open for a specific period should not be revocable within that time.

Is the 'postal rule' appropriate in view of the other means of communication available in the twenty-first century? A person accepting an offer can easily check whether any e-mailed acceptance has been received, possibly using another instantaneous method of communication, such as the telephone. Even when letter post is delivered, it is still possible that letters opened in the front office may not be seen by an intended recipient until much later.

Because some modern methods of communication are considered to be instantaneous, other problems arise. In the *Entores* case, Denning LJ suggested that the burden should rest with the person accepting an offer to make sure his or her communication has been received. For example, if the telephone goes dead, there is a need to telephone again. This approach was approved by the House of Lords in the *Brinkibon* case, and it does seem reasonable to put the onus on the person accepting to check that the acceptance has been received.

The case law on standard form contracts demonstrates the courts' problems in deciding what is offer and what is acceptance.

Consideration

A number of questions need to be considered. Is it fair that something that is not market value can be good consideration? Is it helpful to have a distinction between sufficiency and adequacy? The courts are not interested in whether it is a good or a bad bargain, but simply in whether a bargain exists. Have the rules on past consideration worked fairly? Cases such as *Re McArdle* and *Re Casey's Patents* could be discussed here.

In respect of existing duty rules, the 1990 case of *Williams* v *Roffey* shows that the courts are making real efforts to consider the commercial reality of the situations facing parties in commercial contracts. It seems unlikely, however, following cases such as *Re Selectmove* (1995), that this development will be taken any further.

There is also a problem with promises to accept part-payment of debts. The rule that, without consideration, a promise to accept part-payment is not binding was criticised by the Court of Appeal in *Couldery* v *Bartrum* (1881). Nevertheless, it can be argued in defence of the rule that it protects creditors who are in a weak bargaining position from being forced into accepting less than they are owed.

Both the case of *Williams* v *Roffey* and the law of promissory estoppel (expounded by Denning J in the 1947 case of *Central London Property Trust* v *High Trees House Ltd*) seem to be an attack on the doctrine of consideration, but Professor Atiyah has suggested that if offer, acceptance and intention to create legal relations are all in place, then there is no need for consideration. Promissory estoppel (the principle that if a promisor makes a promise, which another person acts on, the promisor is stopped from breaking the promise, even if the other party did not provide consideration) seems a fair solution to the problem of promises to accept part-payment of debts. However, it is subject to many conditions (for example Birkett LJ said in *Combe* v *Combe* (1951) that it should be 'used as a shield and not as a sword'), and there is some uncertainty about aspects of it.

It remains true that a requirement for consideration allows parties who make promises to escape liability. At the end of the eighteenth century, Lord Mansfield argued that a moral obligation could amount to consideration, but this view was firmly overruled in *Eastwood* v *Kenyon* in 1840. In 1937, the Law Revision Committee proposed reforms to the use of consideration. It suggested that:

- a written promise should always be binding, with or without consideration
- past consideration should be valid
- performance of an existing duty should be good consideration
- a creditor should be bound by a promise to accept part-payment in full settlement of a debt

To date none of these proposals has been adopted.

One reform that has been made is the change introduced by the **Contracts (Rights of Third Parties) Act 1999** affecting third parties who are beneficiaries of contracts — they can now enforce them, even though they have supplied no consideration (see above). This means that cases like *Tweddle* v *Atkinson* would probably be decided differently today.

Intention to create legal relations

Relatively few problems that come before the courts are specifically related to the intention to create legal relations. One reason for this is that many of the situations where it might be relevant are domestic or social so that, often, there is no consideration. It could be argued that there is no need for a separate requirement of intention to create legal relations and that, provided there is valid offer and acceptance, and consideration is present, there is no reason in law why the agreement should not be valid. Feminists have argued that the requirement serves to reinforce the stereotype of the woman in the home not contributing anything of economic value.

A further point that could be made is that the 'binding in honour' exception for football pools agreements does not seem to be justified and can result in unfairness in cases like *Jones* v *Vernons Pools*.

Contract terms

One point that can be made is that the distinction between conditions and warranties is arguably fair because of the emphasis on the relative importance of the term in question. The contrast between the situations in *Bettini* v *Gye* and *Poussard* v *Spiers* would seem to warrant the terms being treated in different ways.

The issue of innominate terms can also be considered. Does the idea of having terms that vary in effect create welcome flexibility or create confusion? The idea clouds the distinction between conditions and warranties and yet it recognises the reality of what parties do in practice and enables the courts to deal with each case on its merits. On the other hand, if terms were fixed in their effect, there would be the advantage of certainty.

The implied terms in the **Sale of Goods Act 1979** and the **Supply of Goods and Services Act 1982** provide important safeguards for consumers, but do the provisions work in a sensible way? Look particularly at the cases dealing with description of goods. Have the courts applied the right balance when interpreting the statutes? Think about the decisions in *Reardon Smith Line* v *Hansen-Tangen*, *Clegg* v *Anderson* (2003) and *Bramhill* v *Edwards*.

Note that the **Supply of Goods and Services Act 1982** provided protection for those hiring goods, and extended the **Sale of Goods Act 1979** implied terms to goods supplied as part of a service, as well as introducing specific terms in respect of services. These are important additions to the rights of consumers. But have the changes made by the **Sale and Supply of Goods Act 1994** improved the protection given to consumers? Section 1(2) states: 'Where the seller sells goods in the course of a business, there is an implied term that the goods supplied under the contract are of satisfactory quality.' This is certainly more easily understood by consumers than was the 'merchantable quality' of which the **Sale of Goods Act 1979** spoke. The 1994 Act also adds some clarification on the meaning of 'satisfactory'.

Acceptance of goods

One significant criticism of the **Sale of Goods Act 1979** was over the issue of acceptance, but s.2(6) of the **Sale and Supply of Goods Act 1994** has since modified the law, stating that the buyer must have a reasonable opportunity to examine goods and that even having something repaired may not amount to acceptance. It seems that simply signing a receipt to acknowledge delivery does not amount to acceptance. However, the courts do not appear to have been entirely consistent in the way they have treated acceptance. Compare *Bernstein* v *Pamson Motors* with *Rogers* v *Parish (Scarborough)*.

Freedom of contract

Is it right that the law should interfere with what the parties have freely contracted to do? Most commentators accept that the protection afforded to consumers is necessary. The original Sale of Goods Act was passed in 1893, at a time when freedom of contract was more of a sacred doctrine than it is today, and the provisions of that original statute were based on rules that had been developed by the common law. Note the current distinction between business and private sales. Is the law right to treat these differently?

Exemption clauses

Look at the common law's treatment of exemption clauses. The emphasis is on incorporation and interpretation, rather than on the clauses' actual merits. Note, however, Denning LJ's effort in *Spurling* v *Bradshaw* to address more fundamental concerns with the 'red hand' rule. The **Unfair Contract Terms Act 1977** seems to have been successful in addressing the issues that the common law was unable to deal with. In particular, it introduced the idea of the consumer sale, allowing the law to offer specific protection to the most vulnerable. It also deals with standard form contracts. But does the Act strike the right balance?

Overlap between the Unfair Contract Terms Act 1977 and the Unfair Terms in Consumer Contracts Regulations 1999

This is an important area to consider. Note that the 1999 Regulations originate from an EU directive and, although they overlap with the provisions of the 1977 Act in some respects, they are wider because they do not just apply to exclusion and limitation clauses. They are narrower, however, in that they apply only to consumer contacts where the terms are not individually negotiated. Because the Regulations and the Act overlap, there is the danger of confusion, especially as the test of unfairness in the Regulations is different from the approach in the Act. The Law Commission report, 'Unfair Terms in Contracts' (2005), recommended the introduction of a single act, replacing the Regulations and the 1977 Act. It also recommended extending to small businesses (in certain circumstances) the protection currently offered to consumers.

Misrepresentation

The **Misrepresentation Act 1967** is a significant improvement on the previous law because, in the past, damages were available only for fraudulent misrepresentation, through the tort of deceit. The only remedy for other kinds of misrepresentation was rescission. As damages and rescission are now available for all types of misrepresentation, distinctions between the types are less significant. The 1967 Act followed the recommendation of the Law Reform Committee that damages should be available for negligent misrepresentation. The effect of s.2(1) is particularly significant, because it allows a claim without having to prove fraud or the special relationship under *Hedley Byrne*. Also under the 1967 Act, the burden of proof was reversed. The defendant must now demonstrate that he or she held a reasonable belief in the truth of the statement. The effect of all these measures is to make it much easier to obtain redress for innocent or negligent misrepresentation.

An evaluation question on misrepresentation would require you to contrast the situation before the 1967 Act with the situation today and to draw attention to the improved remedies available for negligent and innocent misrepresentation. Further guidance is provided in the section on remedies below.

Remedies

Damages are always available as a remedy for all kinds of breach of contract. They are the usual remedy and available as of right where a contract is breached. In many cases it is possible for an award of damages to place the claimant in the same situation as if the contract had been performed. The requirements that the defendant must have caused the breach, that the loss must not be too remote and that the claimant must mitigate his or her loss appear reasonable and ensure fairness between the parties.

Unlike damages, equitable remedies are discretionary and will be awarded by the court only if the circumstances of the case warrant their use. See the section on equitable remedies on pp. 59–60. The remedy of rescission is equitable and therefore discretionary, but it is available for all types of misrepresentation. There are, however, a number of circumstances in which it is not available. Refer back to the section on misrepresentation and consider whether there are circumstances in which non-availability would seem to be reasonable. Before 1964, the only remedy for non-fraudulent misrepresentation was rescission. Damages were not available unless fraud could be proved. This situation was changed by the decision in *Hedley Byrne* (1964), a tort case, and by the **Misrepresentation Act 1967**, which provides a specific remedy of damages, where a remedy would have been available if the misrepresentation had been fraudulent.

Breach of implied terms

The remedies available for breach of implied terms have been strengthened for consumers by the **Sale and Supply of Goods to Consumers Regulations 2002**. Under these regulations, consumers have additional remedies available: repair or replacement of the goods and a partial or full refund. One issue is that a right to reject is lost once the goods have been accepted and the claim would then be limited to damages, which in some situations, for example where the product had malfunctioned several times, would not be as attractive. This issue has already been discussed. Damages are also available as a remedy. Refer back to the chapter on terms and look at the situations where damages would be a better remedy than rejection.

Questions
&
Answers

This section of the guide provides you with questions that cover most of the Unit 3 topics. All the questions are followed by A-grade answers demonstrating both the structured technique that you should adopt and how to use case and statutory authorities effectively.

For 'problem-solving' questions based on a short scenario, the mnemonic **IDEA** may help you with planning and structuring your answers:

I   **Identify** both the appropriate offence(s) and defence(s), or in the case of contract law the appropriate cause(s) of action and defence(s).

D   **Define** the offence(s) and (defences), or cause(s) of action and defence(s).

E   **Explain** the various legal rules.

A   **Apply** these rules to the facts of the question, using authorities (both cases and statutes) to support your answer.

Examiner's comments

The candidate's answers are accompanied by examiner's comments, preceded by the icon ℮. These comments explain the elements of the answer for which marks can be awarded, show why high marks would be given and provide an insight into what examiners are looking for. You are strongly encouraged to download past papers and mark schemes from the AQA website (www.aqa.org.uk) or to obtain these from your teacher.

If you practise adapting the style of the A-grade answers to different question scenarios, it will enable you readily to identify the correct offences (or causes of action) and defences and then to structure your answer effectively using relevant cases and statutes.

Question 1

Non-fatal offence against the person

> Darren and Michael are captains of opposing rugby teams with a history of 'bad blood' between them. These teams are drawn against each other in the semi-final of the regional rugby competition. During this match, Darren tackles Michael as he is about to score a try in injury time. However, the tackle is judged by the referee to be a high one and Darren is sent off the field. As a result of the tackle, Michael's collarbone is fractured and, in falling heavily to the ground, he also loses a tooth.

Discuss Darren's criminal liability for the injuries to Michael. (25 marks)

■ ■ ■

A-grade answer

Given the nature of the injuries that Michael sustained, Darren could be charged with any of three offences under the Offences against the Person Act 1861: grievous bodily harm (GBH) under s.20, wounding (also under s.20) and assault occasioning actual bodily harm (ABH) under s.47. The Joint Charging Standard agreed between the police and Crown Prosecution Service states that broken bones constitute serious injury, which in *R* v *Saunders* was held to define GBH. The loss of the tooth would normally be charged as a s.47 offence but, as bleeding would have been caused, this could equally be charged as wounding under s.20. Wounding was defined in the case of *JCC* v *Eisenhower* (1984) as a breach of both the inner and outer layers of skin.

For both wounding and infliction of GBH under s.20, the *mens rea* is now accepted as being intention or recklessness as to causing some harm, albeit not serious harm. This was established in the case of *R* v *Mowatt* (1967), and confirmed in the case of *R* v *Grimshaw* (1984). It is, therefore, not necessary for the prosecution to seek to prove that the defendant intended GBH or wounding or was reckless as to whether he caused them or not.

In the present case, there can be no doubt that Darren directly caused Michael's injuries — both the 'but for' test for factual causation and the legal rules of causation are clearly satisfied, and it could be strongly argued that the high tackle was at least reckless in the *R* v *Cunningham* sense of 'conscious unjustified risk-taking'. If Darren were to be charged with s.47 assault occasioning ABH for the loss of the tooth, the prosecution would only have to prove that Darren assaulted or battered Michael (inflicting unlawful personal violence), which self-evidently he did, and did so with the *mens rea* of battery — which is intention or subjective recklessness as to the *actus reus* of battery. There is no need for the prosecution to establish that a defendant intended or was reckless as to causing ABH — this important rule was laid down by the House of Lords in the cases of

R v *Savage* and *R* v *Parmenter* (both 1992), and was reaffirmed in *R* v *Roberts.* In the rugby match, the high tackle on Michael by Darren could certainly be described as reckless.

As to defences that Darren could plead, there would appear to be only one — that of consent. This is a limited defence and usually available only in respect of the minor crimes of assault and battery. For the more serious non-fatal offences — ABH and GBH — it can only be successfully pleaded if the activity out of which the injury arises is surgery, including tattooing or body-piercing; rough horseplay; or sport. It is this last category with which we are concerned here. The general rule in contact sports such as rugby is that players are presumed to have consented to serious injuries, provided these occur within the rules of the game. In this case, it is clear from the referee's decision in sending Darren off the field that the tackle constituted foul play; see *R* v *Billinghurst* where the defence of consent was allowed in the case of a rugby match. However, the Court of Appeal in *R* v *Barnes* ruled that criminal prosecutions should only be brought against a sportsperson if his or her conduct was grave enough to be properly categorised as criminal. In the present case, even given the severity of the injury, it is possible that a court would hold that Darren's conduct did not meet the threshold test for a successful prosecution, as high tackles are foreseeable in any rugby match.

> 📝 The candidate immediately refers to the Joint Charging Standard to identify the correct offences and then uses relevant cases to define the *actus reus* and *mens rea.* Since the broken collarbone would certainly be regarded as grievous bodily harm, the loss of a tooth could be treated as wounding, again under s.20. While it is correct to deal with the lost tooth as a s.20 wounding, the candidate would gain additional marks for referring to the Joint Charging Standard at the beginning (which states that the loss of a tooth should be charged under s.47 ABH). Again, both the *actus reus* and *mens rea* elements are correctly described with supporting cases. Students should note how fully the defence of consent is described in this answer. One of the commonest weaknesses in such answers is that defence material is omitted or barely mentioned. This question is comprehensively and accurately answered, with sound use made of relevant case authorities. Out of 25 marks, it would be awarded 21–25.

Question 2

GBH and involuntary manslaughter

Adrian and Brian were in a nightclub, where Adrian took some drugs. Shortly after-wards, Adrian began to act in a strange manner, giggling and stumbling about. When Adrian clumsily spilled a drink over Chris, Brian decided it was time to get him home. As they left the nightclub, they were followed by Chris and his friend Don. Chris challenged Adrian to a fight and Adrian took off his jacket and then immediately lashed out at Chris before Chris was prepared. The blow sent Chris reeling backwards and he dislocated his knee in a very awkward fall.

Meanwhile, Brian had run off but had been caught by Don in a disused building. Don was holding Brian tightly round the neck and causing him to choke, but Brian managed to elbow him twice in the face. Don released his grip, suddenly collapsed, and was sick as he lay on his back. Brian looked at him for a few seconds and then walked away. Don was later found to have died by choking on his vomit.

Adapted from AQA examination paper, June 2002

(a) Discuss Adrian's criminal liability in connection with the injury to Chris.

(25 marks)

(b) Discuss Brian's criminal liability for the involuntary manslaughter of Don.

(25 marks)

■ ■ ■

A-grade answer

(a) In terms of the severity of the injury that Chris sustained — the dislocated knee — Adrian could face a charge under s.20 or s.18 of the Offences against the Person Act 1861. The Joint Charging Standard agreed between the police and Crown Prosecution Service confirms that a dislocated joint should be charged as grievous bodily harm (GBH).

Section 20 requires that the defendant caused GBH to the victim as the *actus reus* of this offence. Grievous bodily harm was defined as 'really serious harm' in *DPP v Smith* (1961), but this was revised to 'serious harm' in *R v Saunders* (1985). As the scenario states that 'Adrian...lashed out at Chris' and 'the blow sent Chris reeling', there would appear to be no difficulty in proving the necessary causation — under both the 'but for' and the legal rules of causation. There was no intervening act between the blow and the injury, and Adrian's action was certainly a 'significant contribution' to the dislocated knee; see *R v Cheshire* (1991).

The *mens rea* of a s.20 offence is now settled as either intention or recklessness to cause some harm. This was decided in *R* v *Mowatt* and confirmed in the case of *R* v *Grimshaw*. It is not, therefore, necessary for the Crown to prove that the defendant intended to cause GBH or was reckless as to whether this would be the outcome. Here, the circumstances clearly suggest that, in starting the fight by lashing out at Chris before he was prepared, Adrian intended to cause at least some harm to Chris.

The *actus reus* of s.18 is identical to that of s.20 — either wounding or GBH. The main difference between these two offences is that of *mens rea*. Section 18 is defined as an offence of specific intent, so to secure a conviction, the Crown must prove that the defendant intended to cause GBH. Intention can be direct (where the defendant had the aim or purpose of causing GBH) or oblique (where the defendant's intent is sufficient if the jury decide he or she foresaw the outcome of GBH as 'virtually certain', as in the cases of *R* v *Nedrick* and *R* v *Woollin*). In this case, even if Adrian could argue he did not wish the actual outcome, nonetheless it is certainly possible for him to be convicted of a s.18 offence, as the action of striking another person so hard that he or she reels backwards and falls could be viewed by the jury as coming within the test laid down in the *Nedrick* and *Woollin* cases. In a case such as Adrian's, where no weapon has been used, it is more usual for the Crown to prosecute on the basis of a s.20 charge.

The defences open to Adrian are limited. It is a clear rule of law that consent cannot be pleaded to ordinary fighting (*R* v *Donovan*), still less to an incident that has resulted in GBH. If he is charged under s.20, Adrian cannot use the defence of intoxication. The cases of *DPP* v *Majewski* and *R* v *Lipman* confirm that voluntary intoxication by drink or drugs can only be pleaded as a partial defence to crimes of specific intent. Section 20 is a basic-intent crime. The defence of automatism, which, if successful, negates the *actus reus* of an offence, is also problematic for Adrian. This defence requires the defendant to prove that, at the time he or she committed the offence, he or she was not in control of his or her actions. Here again, Adrian would face legal difficulties because, for clear policy reasons, the courts are unwilling to allow such a defence if the loss of control has been caused by voluntary intoxication by alcohol or illegal drugs. It is also arguably correct that Adrian was in control of his actions when he attacked Chris because, before doing so, he carefully removed his jacket.

🖉 This is an accurate and well-argued answer where the candidate uses the Joint Charging Standard to identify the appropriate offence. Both *actus reus* and *mens rea* elements are clearly described and supported by case law. The issue of a possible s.18 charge is fully explored but, in the circumstances of the scenario, where no weapon was used, the candidate correctly indicates that a s.20 charge is more likely. The obvious problem with the possible defences to a s.20 charge is that none of them would be successful in the given scenario. The issue of intoxication gives rise to numerous errors in exam answers, but here the issue is decisively dealt with, using the correct cases. This is also true for the defences of consent and automatism. This answer would be awarded 24–25 marks out of 25.

(b) Involuntary manslaughter is defined as unlawful killing without malice aforethought, which is intention to kill or commit GBH. It can be committed in two different ways — by an unlawful and dangerous act or by gross negligence. The former
requires a positive act, which in this case this would be the blows that Brian struck
with his elbow; gross negligence is committed by an omission, which would be
Brian's walking away from Don, who was clearly distressed.

Unlawful and dangerous act manslaughter, also referred to as constructive or
Church doctrine manslaughter, first of all requires that the defendant has committed
a crime — the unlawful act cannot be a tort or contract (*R* v *Franklin*). By striking Don
with his elbows and causing him to collapse, it can be argued that Brian could have
committed GBH, and certainly ABH. The *mens rea* for manslaughter is the *mens rea*
of the unlawful act; if the charge was s.47 ABH or s.20 GBH, the *mens rea* would be
either intention or Cunningham recklessness (conscious taking of an unjustified
risk). As the blows by Brian must have been struck with the intent of causing at least
some harm to Don, the *mens rea* requirement of both offences s.47 and s.20 is satisfied, and accordingly Brian has the necessary *mens rea* for manslaughter.

The second requirement is that the unlawful act must also be dangerous. In *Church*
(confirmed by *DPP* v *Newbury and Jones*), this was defined as 'dangerous in the sense
that a sober and reasonable person would recognise that the act carried the risk of
some harm albeit not serious injury'. The use of an elbow to strike the victim twice
in the face would certainly satisfy this limited test.

The final test is that the unlawful act must have caused the death of the victim (*R* v
Goodfellow). Here, Brian's attack satisfies both the factual 'but for' test of causation
and the legal rules established in *R* v *Smith* and *R* v *Cheshire*. His attack was both the
substantial and operating cause of death and a significant contribution to Don's
death.

It can therefore be strongly argued that Brian has both the *actus reus* and *mens rea*
of unlawful and dangerous act manslaughter.

In respect of his omission in walking away from Don, who was clearly seriously ill
having collapsed and been sick, Brian could be liable for manslaughter by gross
negligence. This is based on the civil tort of negligence and requires there to be a
duty of care, the breach of which causes the victim's death, and gross negligence
that the jury believes makes the act criminal and thus deserving of punishment. The
issue of duty of care relies on the incremental tests established in *Caparo* v *Dickman*
— foreseeability of harm, proximity and the policy test of whether it is fair, just and
reasonable to impose a duty of care. Here, it could be argued that having struck Don
and caused his collapse, the reasonable person would foresee some further harm,
and there is clearly proximity in terms of time and space. There is also no policy
reason why a duty should not be imposed. It could also be alleged that by walking
away in these circumstances, Brian breached his duty of care — this test is also an
objective test based on the 'reasonable man'. The issue of causation has already
been addressed above.

The final issue, that of gross negligence itself, is one for the jury to decide upon. In the leading case of *Adomako*, Lord Mackay declined to define what gross negligence meant, choosing to leave this to the jury as he felt that such a definition would be incomprehensible. However, in *R v Singh*, the trial judge laid down the following test for the jury: 'The question posed is having regard to the risk of death involved, was the defendant's conduct so bad in all the circumstances as to amount in your judgement to a criminal act or omission?' This direction was later approved by the Court of Appeal.

Lord Taylor CJ in *Adomako* had suggested that 'inattention or failure to address a serious risk which goes beyond mere carelessness in respect of an obvious matter which the defendant's duty demanded he should address' could properly lead a jury to make a finding of gross negligence.

In the light of these legal rulings, Brian could be convicted of gross negligence manslaughter, but it remains much more likely on the facts of this case that he would be convicted of unlawful and dangerous act manslaughter.

In his defence, Brian could plead self-defence. It is the position under both common law and statute — s.3 of the Criminal Law Act 1967 — that a person if attacked is entitled to protect himself by using such force as is reasonable in all the circumstances. Where justified, this can provide a complete defence by negating the unlawfulness of the homicide or assault — in effect, this defence renders the circumstances that surround the act not unlawful. Given that Don 'was holding Brian tightly round the neck and causing him to choke', it could be argued that Brian's reaction of elbowing him twice in the face was both a proportionate and reasonable use of force.

📝 This answer is well structured and clear. The introductory paragraph both defines the offence effectively and 'lays out' the structure of the response in terms of both types of involuntary manslaughter that need to be addressed. The rules of unlawful act manslaughter are fully explained and applied with good use of relevant case authorities. Students should note how the issue of *mens rea* for this offence is dealt with, as often the *mens rea* is virtually ignored. The rules concerning gross negligence manslaughter are also clearly explained and applied, with emphasis laid on the *Singh* direction and the relevant example of gross negligence drawn from Lord Talyor's judgement in *Adomako*. Finally, the issue of self-defence is dealt with effectively.

This answer would receive **24 out of the 25 marks** available.

Question 3

Critical evaluation of law on non-fatal offences

Critically analyse the present law on non-fatal offences. (25 marks)

■ ■ ■

A-grade answer

The first observation to be made about the law on non-fatal offences is that it is not completely codified. The separate offences of assault and battery remain common law offences, albeit with their separate nature confirmed in s.39 of the Criminal Justice Act 1988, but the more serious offences — assault occasioning actual bodily harm (ABH), wounding and inflicting grievous bodily harm (GBH) and causing GBH with intent are contained in the Offences against the Person Act 1861.

Even at the time of its passing into law, the 1861 Act was rightly described as 'a rag-bag of offences' by its own draftsman, and as it is now nearly 150 years old, the criticisms are even more acute. Some of the language used is now archaic — 'grievous bodily harm' simply means serious harm, and 'assault occasioning actual bodily harm' most commonly means some kind of battery causing real harm to a victim. As to case law, the definition given to 'wounding' in *JCC* v *Eisenhower* (any breach in the outer and inner layers of the skin) is far too wide, as it could cover anything from a minor cut or even a graze. An interesting contrast can be made here with regard to the Theft Act 1968, which was intended to codify the entire law of theft. Within 10 years, a further Theft Act had to be passed and there have been significant statutory additions and amendments since. Yet the 1861 Act remains unamended (except by judicial interventions).

Other linguistic criticisms arise over the words 'assault' and 'battery'. Although 'assault' is technically used to describe 'causing a victim to fear the use of unlawful personal violence', it is most commonly understood to refer to some sort of physical attack. The strict definition of 'battery' is 'unlawful touching' and no injury of any sort is required.

Probably the most serious criticism of the 1861 Act concerns the issue of *mens rea* for each of the offences. Section 47, which deals with assault occasioning ABH, is entirely silent on the issue of *mens rea*, and it has been left to the courts to determine what it is. The cases of *R* v *Savage* and *R* v *Parmenter* now confirm that the *mens rea* of assault or battery — intention or subjective recklessness — is all that is required. In s.20, the word 'malicious' has been interpreted to mean 'intention or recklessness as to causing some harm' (*R* v *Mowatt* and *R* v *Grimshaw*). In interpreting s.18, judges and academic

lawyers have concluded that 'malicious' is effectively redundant, except as regards the secondary *mens rea* — intent to resist arrest.

A further point of criticism is that this Act is now undergoing almost perpetual revision and rewriting by judges, which could almost be called 'law-making by statutory interpretation'. The 2003 case of *R v Dica*, which involved a defendant being convicted of 'biological' GBH under s.20 after infecting two women with HIV, is another good example of the ability of senior courts to amend the law. The Court of Appeal, having quashed his conviction and ordered a retrial, confirmed that injury by reckless infection does constitute a s.20 offence and that *R v Clarence* (where a husband was prosecuted for infecting his wife with gonorrhoea) was overruled on the issue of direct bodily violence being required. (The more significant part of this judgement relates to the defence of consent, as the court ruled that if the victims knew or suspected that the defendant was infected, no criminal liability would arise.)

Given the judicial decisions in *R v Savage* (s.47) and *R v Mowatt* (s.20), it is clear that these two offences now involve constructive liability — making it unnecessary for the Crown to prove intention or recklessness as to the *actus reus* of the offence. A conviction under s.47 can be obtained by proving that ABH was in fact caused by common assault and that the defendant either intended or was reckless as to the assault or battery. For neither of the offences is there a need to prove that the defendant intended or was reckless as to causing any level of harm at all. This issue of constructive liability militates against a basic principle of criminal liability called the principle of correspondence, which requires that the *mens rea* should be related to the *actus reus* of the offence and to the possible consequences of being convicted of that offence.

Finally, the 'hierarchy of sentencing' can easily be criticised. Both assault and battery have the same maximum sentence — 6 months. Section 47 ABH (for which only 'any hurt or injury which interferes with the health or comfort of the victim' needs to be proved) carries a maximum sentence 10 times that level — 5 years — which is exactly the same as that for s.20 wounding and inflicting GBH. These maximum sentences lack even a semblance of consistency or coherence.

It is evident that there is an indisputable case for the complete codification of the law on all non-fatal offences, but even the Law Commission's 1994 recommendations for reform did not include the common law offences of assault and battery. Although those recommendations have been welcomed by all governments since, no action has been taken to incorporate them into any of the major Criminal Justice Acts passed since.

> This answer is both comprehensive and well argued. All the major issues are addressed: the archaic and confusing language, the much criticised issue of constructive liability, the inconsistency of sentencing levels and the delay in implementing law reform. Key cases are used effectively to illustrate the various points of criticism. Reference to the topical and important case of *R v Dica* is particularly useful. This answer would be awarded full marks.

Question 1

Misrepresentation and breach of contract

Laura decided that she needed to lose some weight, so she paid £100 to Nell for ten 'weight loss' sessions. Nell's promotional material proclaimed her to be very experienced in running such sessions. It quoted a number of former participants as having been astonished and delighted by their weight losses. In fact, Nell was very much a beginner and she had made up the favourable quotes. After three sessions, Laura was dissatisfied with Nell's disorganised approach and unhelpful advice, and she decided that she wanted all of her money back.

Adapted from AQA examination paper, January 2006

Having regard to the rules on misrepresentation and breach, consider the rights, duties and remedies of Laura and of Nell. (25 marks)

■ ■ ■

A-grade answer

Nell's statements appear to be a misrepresentation, which is regarded in contract law as a vitiating factor, i.e. one that may invalidate the consent required for a contract to be binding. For a misrepresentation to be actionable, it has to fulfil three requirements:

- it must be untrue
- it must be a statement of fact not opinion (*Bissett* v *Wilkinson* 1927)
- it must have induced the innocent party to enter into the contract

In the present case, it is immediately clear that the statements in the promotional material were untrue and it is equally clear that they purported to be statements of fact. They claimed that Nell was experienced in running weight-loss sessions, whereas she was in reality a beginner, and the quotes of former participants were invented.

There must be evidence that the misrepresentation induced the other party to enter the contract. In this case, it is difficult to see how Laura could have checked the truth of the statements. She quite clearly relied on them and she had no alternative source of information to use.

Contract law recognises three types of misrepresentation — fraudulent, negligent and innocent. Which category a misrepresentation falls into depends on the state of mind of the person making the statement. Fraudulent misrepresentation, also actionable as the tort of deceit, was defined in *Derry* v *Peek* as a false statement 'that is made (i) knowingly, or (ii) without belief in its truth, or (iii) recklessly as to whether it be true or false'. Negligent misrepresentation was established in the leading case of *Hedley Byrne* v *Heller Partners Ltd*, which established that a duty of care is created where there is a

'special relationship' between the parties and reliance is placed by one party on a state-ment given by the other. Today, however, the Misrepresentation Act 1967 is used much more widely in cases of negligent misrepresentation. In Nell's case, it is evident that the statements amounted to fraudulent misrepresentation because they had been deliber-ately invented. They were made in the full knowledge that they were false and so meet the criteria for fraudulent misrepresentation set out in *Derry* v *Peek*.

The effect of a misrepresentation is generally to make the contract voidable, so that it continues to exist unless and until the innocent party chooses to have it set aside by means of rescission, an equitable remedy, which puts the parties back in the position they were in before the contract was made. Rescission will not be ordered where it is impossible to return the parties to their original pre-contract position.

Affirmation of the contract, which means saying or doing something to indicate an intention to continue with it, is a bar to rescission. With fraudulent misrepresentation, however, the right to rescind will not be lost through what appears to be affirmation if the innocent party was not aware of the fraud and could not have been expected to dis-cover it with reasonable diligence, because he or she would not have known that there was any right to rescind (*Peyman* v *Lanjani*, 1985). Laura did attend three sessions, which might indicate an intention to affirm the contract, but it could be argued that this was before her gradual dissatisfaction with Nell's performance gave her the idea that the promotional material might be fraudulent; she should not, therefore, lose the right to rescind.

Laura can also claim damages as a result of the misrepresentation for any losses (i.e. the £100 she has paid), which she has suffered as a direct consequence of it. Damages for misrepresentation are calculated on the same basis as they are in tort, so that the aim is to put the parties back in the position they were in before the misrepresentation was made.

It can be argued that Nell is in breach of contract because of her disorganised approach and unhelpful advice. Assuming that this does amount to a breach, Laura's rights will depend on the nature of the term that has been broken. A breach of a condition is a breach of an important term and gives the right to terminate the agreement and repu-diate (cancel) the contract. Where the injured party elects to repudiate for a breach of condition, the general effect is to terminate the contract from the date of that election. A breach of warranty is a breach of a minor term that does not go to the root of the con-tract and gives rise only to a claim for damages. The distinction between conditions and warranties is illustrated by the 1876 cases of *Bettini* v *Gye* and *Poussard* v *Spiers and Pond*.

If Laura is able to establish that the breach went to the very root of the agreement and amounted to a breach of condition, she will be able to recover all the money paid, including that for future sessions because she will be able to cancel the contract. How-ever, if the court decides that the disorganisation and unhelpful advice amount only to breach of warranty, Laura will be able to claim only compensation for the poor quality of the sessions, which will probably be a proportion of the £30 paid for the three sessions she has had. She would not be entitled to cancel the sessions still to come, even though she may by now be unwilling to continue with the course

🖉 This is a well-structured answer, dealing effectively with both breach and misrepresentation. The rules on misrepresentation are explained thoroughly and the different types distinguished. Notice how the answer refers frequently to the circumstances outlined in the question and applies the rules to reach a conclusion. The section on breach is briefer, but the important elements are identified and applied to the facts. Candidates often neglect to deal with remedies in sufficient depth, but this answer outlines all the remedies available and considers the different possibilities that may arise. It is a strong response and would merit 23 marks out of a total of 25.

section

Question 2

Frustration and breach of contract

Sue asked Paul to create a large banner to be the centrepiece of a forthcoming protest march on the theme of 'exploitation of animals through the ages'. She agreed to pay him £2,000 in total, £200 immediately and the remainder on completion and delivery of the banner. One month before delivery was due, Sue 'cancelled' the agreement because of financial difficulties and told Paul that she would not pay for the banner. By that time, the banner was almost finished and Paul had spent £400 on materials. He refused to accept the 'cancellation' and continued to work on the banner. A week before delivery was due, an order was made prohibiting all marches in the locality for 1 month because of fears that the protest march would provoke violence and disorder. In consequence, the protest march had to be abandoned.

Adapted from AQA examination paper, January 2006

Having regard to the rules on breach and frustration in contracts, consider the rights, duties and remedies of Paul and of Sue. (25 marks)

■ ■ ■

A-grade answer

Sue seems to be in breach of contract when she 'cancels' the agreement. Her conduct amounts to anticipatory breach and Paul would be entitled to treat the contract as at an end and sue for damages. However, he opts to continue with the work. The injured party in an anticipatory breach of contract does have this option and can then sue for breach later, when the performance date has passed. This is what happened in *Avery* v *Bowden*, a case involving an agreement to supply a cargo for a ship at a port in Russia. Unfortunately, by the time the cargo was due, the contract had become frustrated because of the outbreak of the Crimean War, which made trading with Russia illegal. Paul could face a similar outcome if the court decides that the contract has been frustrated by the banning of the march. The issue of frustration is discussed later in this answer.

The innocent party may not always be able to insist on affirming the contract because, under the principle of mitigation of loss, he or she usually has a general duty to take reasonable steps to minimise the loss. In *White and Carter* v *McGregor* (1962), the claimants opted to affirm the contract and the court upheld this decision, but added the provisos that it must be possible to carry out the contract without the other party's cooperation and that there must be a 'legitimate interest' in carrying on with the contract. In the present situation, it is possible for Paul to continue with the work without Sue's cooperation, and he would probably argue that there is a legitimate interest because there was not much he could have done to mitigate his loss, as the materials had already been bought and most of the work was already done. He should, therefore, be able to claim the full £2,000, provided he completes the banner and delivers it on time.

Sue may argue, however, that the contract has been frustrated because, a week before the banner was due to be delivered, an order was made prohibiting the march, of which the banner was to be the centrepiece. Frustration arises when an event occurs during the lifetime of a contract that is not the fault of either party and that makes completion of the contract impossible, illegal or radically different. The substance of the agreement itself has to be undermined and it is not sufficient that completion is made more difficult or expensive. A contract can also be frustrated if it is rendered impossible by the passing of a new statute, which makes the provisions of the contract illegal. This is not exactly the situation here. It is true that the march has been banned, but only for a month, and the banner would presumably be equally relevant to future marches in a few months' time. *Herne Bay Steam Boat* v *Sutton* is relevant here. Arguably, the banner continues to have a purpose even without the march. It could be displayed on other occasions and in a variety of circumstances. Given the fact that it cost £2,000, it seems unlikely that Sue intended it to be destroyed immediately after the march and never used again. Her claim of frustration of contract seems unlikely to succeed, especially if the court takes account of the fact that she attempted to cancel the contract before the march had been banned. If it did succeed, however, Sue would be in a much better position than if she were in breach of contract. Under the Law Reform (Frustrated Contracts) Act 1943, all money is returned to where it was originally, allowing the court to apportion losses fairly between the parties so that they can each be reimbursed for expenses or for goods or services already obtained under the contract.

The issue here would be whether Sue has obtained a valuable benefit. One of the problems is to decide whether the valuable benefit is the work itself or the end product. In this case, the banner could be seen as valuable in itself and Sue will have the benefit of it in the future. It is possible, therefore, that, even if the contract is held to be frustrated, Sue will have to pay a substantial proportion of the £1,800 due on delivery of the banner in recognition of the valuable benefit she has obtained.

> This is a thorough and detailed answer, which outlines the relevant rules on both breach and frustration and makes good use of case authority. Notice how the answer uses the cases that seem to be the most relevant and applies them to the contract between Sue and Paul. Notice, too, how frequently the answer refers to the facts in the question. To get high marks, answers must outline relevant rules and apply them to the situation described in the scenario. This response would score 23 out of 25 marks.

section

Question 3

Offer and acceptance

Ulric wanted to sell a box of tools in which he knew that Vernon, his friend, was interested. He left a message on Vernon's home telephone answering machine saying: 'The tools are yours for £70. Tell me "yes" or "no" by Tuesday. Leave a message if I am out.' Later that day, Vernon sent a text message to Ulric's mobile phone telling him that he would buy the tools. Ulric did not see the message until Friday. On Wednesday, Ulric put an advertisement in the window of a local shop, which stated: 'Great offer. Box of tools — £80.' On Thursday, Wayne rang Ulric and asked whether he would accept £60 for the tools, which Ulric refused. Wayne then rang Ulric again, on Friday, shortly after Ulric had seen Vernon's message, and said that he would pay £80. Five minutes later, Yan rang Ulric and offered £90 for the tools.

Adapted from AQA examination paper, January 2007

Having regard to the relevant rules on formation of contracts, consider whether Ulric is legally entitled to accept Yan's offer of £90 for the box of tools. (25 marks)

■ ■ ■

A-grade answer

The issue is whether Ulric is free to accept Yan's offer or already contractually bound to sell the tools to Vernon or Wayne. Dealing first with Vernon, it is necessary to identify whether there is offer and acceptance. An offer can be defined as an expression of willingness to contract on certain terms, made with the intention that it will become binding on acceptance. It needs to be distinguished from an invitation to treat, which is an invitation to someone to make an offer.

To be an offer, the terms must be certain and unambiguous. In *Guthing v Lynn* (1831), the buyer of a horse promised to pay the seller an extra £5 'if the horse is lucky for me'. This was considered too vague to constitute an offer. The offer must be communicated so that its terms are known to the person accepting, and finally it must still be in existence when it is accepted. Ulric's statement, 'The tools are yours for £70. Tell me "yes" or "no" by Tuesday. Leave a message if I am out', would seem to meet all these conditions and constitute an offer. Ulric is entitled to attach conditions in respect of acceptance, but there is perhaps a degree of ambiguity, in that he asks for an answer by Tuesday and yet an answer-phone message, left on Tuesday, might not be picked up until later.

To be valid, an acceptance must be an unqualified and unconditional agreement by words or conduct to all the terms of the offer. It is not clear whether Vernon attempts to speak directly to Ulric, but he does send an unambiguous acceptance by text message 'later that day', which seems to be well within the deadline of Tuesday. It could be argued that, by saying 'Leave a message if I am out', Ulric is expecting a message on his home telephone, but this is not explicit and Vernon can certainly argue that he has left a message.

It is clear from *Tinn* v *Hoffman* that, even though Ulric may have contemplated a telephone call to a landline, any method by which the answer was received on Tuesday would have sufficed. This may mean that the mobile phone text message would not suffice, given that there was no certainty that it would have been seen in time. Arguably, Vernon has failed to communicate his acceptance and so the offer to him is terminated.

Another issue in respect of the offer to Vernon is whether, in view of the fact that they were friends, there was an intention to create legal relations. The presumption that the arrangement is a purely social one will be rebutted if money has changed hands. The leading cases involving people other than family members — among them *Simpkins* v *Pays* (1955), *Peck* v *Lateu* (1973) and *Parker* v *Clarke* (1960) — suggest that the courts will treat agreements between friends as contractual, so long as the actions of the parties suggest that they intended to form a legal agreement. This would seem to be the case here, because Ulric's conduct suggests that he was willing to sell to anyone who would pay the price he was asking.

In respect of the negotiations with Wayne, Ulric's advertisement in the window of the shop would probably constitute an invitation to treat. It is clear that small advertisements, for example in magazines or newspapers, are treated as invitations on the ground that there may be further bargaining about details such as price (*Partridge* v *Crittenden*). Wayne is probably making a counter-offer when he asks whether Ulric will accept £60, and it is evident from *Hyde* v *Wrench* that the effect of this is to end Ulric's offer to Wayne. It is also possible that Wayne was merely requesting further information rather than making an offer. Requests for further information are classed as invitations to treat. In fact, it does not make any difference because Ulric is clearly not prepared to accept an offer or prepared to invite an offer at that price. Wayne then makes a new offer of £80, which Ulric is free to accept or reject.

We are not told what Ulric's response was, but, assuming that he does not accept this offer, and assuming that he does not have a binding contract with Vernon, then he is free to accept the offer which Yan then makes.

> The question sets out quite a complicated series of events and it is important when answering questions like this to take time to clarify all the relevant issues and work out where each event fits in. Notice how this response begins by looking at the negotiations with Wayne and Vernon because, although the question asks about the offer from Yan, this cannot be properly considered without deciding whether or not there is already a contract with Wayne or Vernon.
>
> The answer refers to relevant rules on both offer and acceptance, but is selective in the rules it details, concentrating on those that have a bearing on the situation being

discussed. Frequent reference is made to the facts in the question and the candidate avoids the danger of simply listing the rules with little application. A possible criticism is that this answer deals rather briefly with the rules and concentrates on application, but it is a relevant and well-argued discussion and would merit at least 22 marks out of 25.

Question 4

Sale of Goods Act, exclusion clauses and privity of contract

Harry bought a £500 bicycle from Norman's Bikes as a birthday present for his nephew, Ian. Harry told Norman that it was for Ian, and supplied Ian's name and address for delivery. The invoice contained a clause stating that Norman would have the right to repair or replace any defective item at his sole discretion, and limiting his liability for any loss arising out of defects in the bicycle to the cost of the bicycle itself. A few weeks later, when Ian was riding the bicycle, the metal in the front forks fractured, throwing him over the handlebars and onto the pavement. As a result of his injuries, he was off work for two weeks and lost £600 in wages.

Adapted from AQA specimen examination paper

Consider Ian's rights and remedies, if any, against Norman in connection with the sale of the bicycle and the financial loss suffered on account of his injuries. (25 marks)

■ ■ ■

A-grade answer

This is a contract for the sale of goods, and the implied terms in the Sale of Goods Act 1979 are therefore applicable to it. Under s.14(2) there is an implied term that goods are of satisfactory quality. This term applies only to sales in the course of a business and not to private sales, but they will apply to this sale because Norman's Bikes is clearly a business. Under Section 14(2)(a), goods are satisfactory if 'they meet the standard that a reasonable person would regard as satisfactory, taking account of any description of the goods, the price (if relevant) and all other relevant circumstances'. In *Bartlett* v *Sidney Marcus* (1965), the court said that a second-hand car did not have to be in perfect condition and some defects were to be expected. However, the bike in this question appears to be new and Harry has paid £500, which does not seem to be a reduced price. He would therefore expect it to be without defect.

Among the potentially relevant factors outlined under s.14(2)(b) to determine what is meant by satisfactory quality are safety and durability. In *Priest* v *Last*, a hot-water bottle burst. It was clearly neither safe nor durable. Here we are told that, after Ian had ridden the bike for a few weeks, the metal in the front forks fractured. This would suggest that the bike is not durable because metal should not fracture after such a short period. The fracture led to an accident and so the bike, like the hot-water bottle in *Priest* v *Last*, is not safe and therefore not of satisfactory quality.

Section 14(3) states that there is an implied term that goods are fit for any purpose specifically made known to the seller, unless the buyer does not rely on the seller's judgement or it would be unreasonable for him or her to do so. There is no suggestion in this case that that the bike was being used for an unusual purpose and therefore there is an expectation that it is fit for the purpose for which bikes are normally sold. There would, therefore, be a breach of s.14(2) as well as s.14(3), as there was in *Priest* v *Last*.

We are also told that the invoice contained a clause stating that Norman would have the right to repair or replace any defective item at his sole discretion, and limiting his liability for any loss arising out of defects in the bicycle to the cost of the bicycle itself. Under s.6 of the Unfair Contract Terms Act 1977, the terms in s.14 of the Sale of Goods Act 1979 cannot be excluded from consumer contracts. Applying s.12(1) of the 1977 Act, Harry is clearly buying as a consumer, so any limitation clause cannot exclude the implied terms and restrict the remedies that would be available for a breach of implied terms. Because the implied terms are conditions, Harry has the right to the reject the contract as well as to claim damages, so the clause stating that Norman has the right to determine the remedy is invalid. However under s.11(4) of the 1979 Act, this right to reject is lost once the goods have been accepted and the claim would then be limited to damages.

In this case it is unclear whether the goods would be treated as accepted, but, in any event, the claim here will also involve damages, which will always be a remedy, whether the goods have been accepted or not. Damages are appropriate where, as in this case, consumers have suffered personal injury because of a faulty product and wish to sue for consequential loss. The consumer will often be awarded sums far exceeding the value of the product itself, for example in *Godley* v *Perry* £2,500 was awarded for the loss of an eye caused by a faulty catapult. The claim here would be for loss of earnings.

The final issue that needs to be discussed is the fact that it is Ian who is injured, rather than the purchaser of the bike. Only parties to a contract can sue under it and Ian is not a party to the contract for purchase of the bike. However, the Contracts (Rights of Third Parties) Act 1999 creates certain exceptions to the general rule of privity of contract. Under s.1(1), the Act allows a third party to enforce a contract if it contains an express term to that effect or if it purports to confer a benefit on him or her. The Act allows enforcement only where the benefit is intended for a specific person or for a member of a specific group and where it is clear that the parties intended the benefit to be enforceable by the third party. We are told that Harry told Norman that the bike was for Ian, and supplied Ian's name and address for delivery. The provisions of the Act would therefore apply and Ian will be able to sue under the contract.

There are a number of different issues to be considered in this question. It requires discussion of the Sale of Goods Act implied terms, the remedies available under the Act and the issue of acceptance. Notice how the answer covers these elements and how effectively it uses case authority to try to assess how the rules would be applied. The answer also has to consider the impact of the limitation clause, but coverage is brief because there are so many other issues to discuss. Finally, the answer has to deal with the fact that it is Ian who is injured while using the bike, when he was not a party to the contract. A lot is expected of candidates on this question, and in the time available, it is difficult to see how an answer could cover much more than this response does. It would be awarded full marks.

Question 5

Critical evaluation of law on offer and acceptance

**What criticisms would you make of the rules on formation of contracts?
Relate your answer to the rules on offer and acceptance.** (25 marks)

■ ■ ■

A-grade answer

The rules on offer and acceptance have been developed by the courts over many years, and the fact that there has been no need for statutory intervention suggests that, on the whole, they have worked well. However, there are a number of criticisms that can be made of specific aspects.

One long-standing concern is the relationship between offers and invitations to treat. An offer can be defined as an expression of willingness to contract on certain terms, made with the intention that it will become binding on acceptance. On the face of it, goods advertised in shop windows would seem to comply with this definition. However, goods in shop windows are invitations to treat, not offers. The case of *Fisher* v *Bell* — where a shopkeeper was prosecuted for displaying an illegal flick-knife for sale in his shop window and acquitted because an exhibition of goods in a shop window is not an offer for sale — illustrates the confusion this can cause. It could be argued that the outcome was unsatisfactory because the shopkeeper clearly intended to sell the knife and he would have sold it to anyone who came in with the right money. Equally clearly, Parliament intended to criminalise exactly this kind of behaviour.

One consequence of the current law on offers and invitations is that, in retail situations, the seller retains ultimate control over who to sell to. This is based on the principle of freedom of contract, and Professor Sir Percy Winfield made a case for it in a 1939 article in the *Law Quarterly Review*, arguing that 'a shop is a place for bargaining and not compulsory sales'. Decisions such as *Pharmaceutical Society* v *Boots* follow this principle.

There is still confusion in some areas, for example with timetables and tickets for transport. In *Wilkie* v *London Passenger Transport Board* (1947), it was suggested that the offer is made by running the service, and acceptance is when the passenger gets on board, but in *Contract Law* Elliott and Quinn suggest that, if the principles laid down in *Thornton* v *Shoe Lane Parking* (1971) are followed, it would appear that passengers asking for a ticket are making an invitation to treat, that the bus company makes an offer by issuing the ticket and that the passenger accepts the offer by keeping the ticket without objection.

Another area of potential difficulty is distinguishing offers from responses to requests for further information. In *Harvey* v *Facey*, it was held that, following the appellants' telegram to Facey, reading 'Will you sell us Bumper Hall Pen? Telegraph lowest cash price — answer paid', Facey's reply (a telegram reading 'Lowest price for Bumper Hall Pen £900') was not an offer but merely a statement of the price. The courts have adopted quite a narrow interpretation of what constitutes an offer when information is being supplied. For example, in *Gibson* v *Manchester City Council* (1979), a statement that the council 'may be prepared to sell the house to you' at a certain price was held to be an invitation to treat, not an offer.

Acceptance in unilateral contracts is another difficulty because acceptance can be through conduct, so it may not always be clear when performance constituting acceptance has started. Where a substantial amount of work has been done by an offeree, it would not seem fair to allow the offeror to revoke the offer. As a solution to this, the Law Commission in 1975 suggested that an offer that the offeror has said will be open for a specific period should not be revocable within that period.

There is also the issue of the 'postal rule', which applies when ordinary letter post is used and means that acceptance is valid when posted, even if the letter is lost in the post, but a revocation of an offer is valid only when it is received. These days, fewer and fewer contracts are being entered into by letter, so the postal rule will become less relevant, but there may still be situations — such as delivery by courier — where it would apply. The main problem with the postal rule is that the offeror may not know of the acceptance, for example if the letter disappears in the post. In *Re London and Northern Bank* (1900), it was held that a letter is posted if it is correctly addressed and stamped and placed in an official post box; this at least suggests that an incorrectly addressed letter would not constitute acceptance.

The broader issue is whether the postal rule is any longer appropriate in view of the other means of communication now available. In the twenty-first century, a person accepting an offer can easily check whether any e-mailed or posted acceptance has been received, possibly using an instantaneous method of communication, such as the telephone or fax. It would be more consistent to have a rule that makes acceptance valid only when it is received. Another issue is that, even when it is delivered, a letter opened in the front office may not be seen by an intended recipient until much later.

Further problems relating to acceptance arise with the use of electronic communications, which are transmitted instantaneously. Denning LJ in the *Entores* case suggested that the burden should rest with the person accepting the offer to make sure that his or her communication has been received. For example, if the telephone goes dead, there is a need to telephone again.

✐ This is a thorough answer and discusses a range of issues. Notice that it concentrates heavily on evaluation and refers to the rules only when an evaluative comment is made. The danger with this question is that the answer may become a summary of the rules, with little evaluative comment. This answer avoids that trap, and would be awarded 22–23 marks out of 25.

PHILIP ALLAN
UPDATES

Student Unit Guides

There are guides to help you
in the following subjects:

Accounting (AQA)

Biology (AQA, Edexcel, OCR)

Business Studies (AQA, Edexcel,
OCR)

Chemistry (AQA, Edexcel, OCR (A),
OCR (B) (Salters))

Economics (AQA, Edexcel, OCR)

English Language (AQA)

English Language and Literature
(AQA)

Geography (AQA, Edexcel, OCR)

Government & Politics (AQA,
Edexcel, OCR)

History (Edexcel, OCR)

Law (AQA, OCR)

Mathematics (AQA, Edexcel, OCR)

Media Studies (AQA, OCR)

Physical Education (AQA, Edexcel,
OCR)

Physics (Edexcel, OCR)

Psychology (AQA (A), (AQA (B),
Edexcel, OCR)

Sociology (AQA, OCR)

■ Focus your revision

■ Build your confidence

■ Strengthen your exam technique

Visit **www.philipallan.co.uk** for the full list of unit guides and to order online,
or telephone our Customer Services Department on **01235 827720**

PHILIP ALLAN
UPDATES

AQA Law

Ian Yule, Peter Darwent & Jennifer Currer

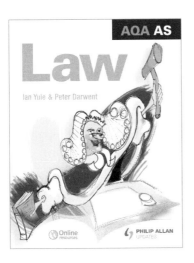

- Accessible and up-to-date coverage of the new specification
- Examiner's advice on how to approach topics and avoid common pitfalls
- Frequent definition of key concepts and terms, and summaries of the latest legal developments
- Sample questions and answers

For more information and to order online, visit **www.philipallan.co.uk**, or telephone our Customer Services Department on **01235 827720**